A Walk through Rebel Dublin 1916

Mick O'Farrell

ⲘERCIER PRESS

Rebel Commander-in-Chief
PH Pearse

British Commander-in-Chief
Sir John Maxwell

⅏ERCIER PRESS

First published in 1999 by
Mercier Press
5 French Church Street Cork
Tel: (021) 275040; Fax (021) 274969
E-mail: books@mercier.ie
16 Hume Street Dublin 2
Tel: (01) 661 5299; Fax: (01) 661 8583
E-mail: books@marino.ie

Trade enquiries to CMD Distribution
55A Spruce Avenue
Stillorgan Industrial Park
Blackrock County Dublin
Tel: (01) 294 2556; Fax: (01) 294 2564
E-mail: cmd@columba.ie

© Mick O'Farrell 1999
Contemporary photographs (except on pages 23 & 87) © Denis O'Farrell

ISBN 1 85635 276 5

10 9 8 7 6 5 4 3 2 1
A CIP record for this title is available from the British Library

Layout, cover design, photo re-touching by Mick O'Farrell

Printed in Ireland by ColourBooks,
Baldoyle Industrial Estate, Dublin 13.

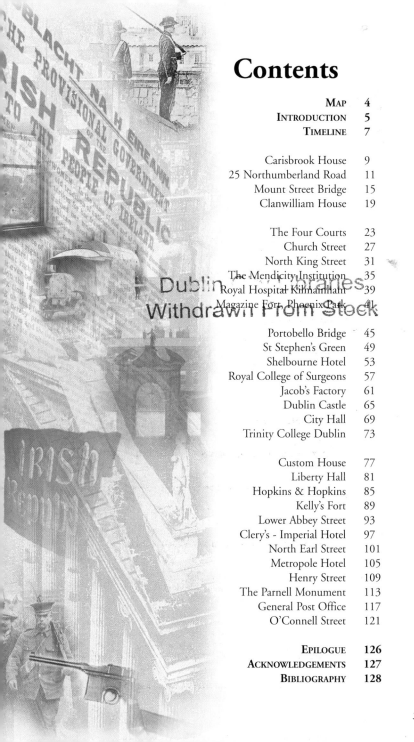

Contents

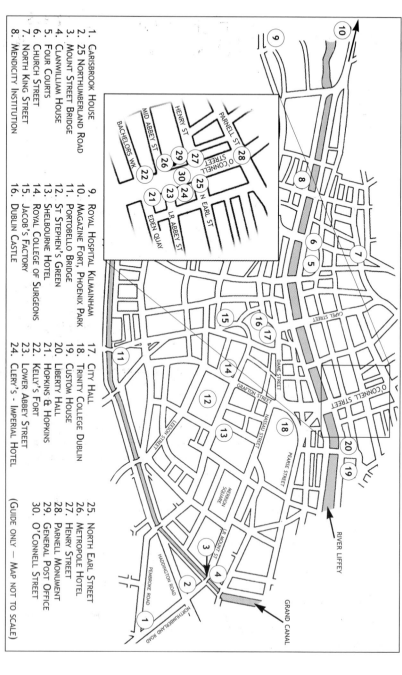

1. CARISBROOK HOUSE
2. 25 NORTHUMBERLAND ROAD
3. MOUNT STREET BRIDGE
4. CLANWILLIAM HOUSE
5. FOUR COURTS
6. CHURCH STREET
7. NORTH KING STREET
8. MENDICITY INSTITUTION

9. ROYAL HOSPITAL KILMAINHAM
10. MAGAZINE FORT, PHOENIX PARK
11. PORTOBELLO BRIDGE
12. ST STEPHEN'S GREEN
13. SHELBOURNE HOTEL
14. ROYAL COLLEGE OF SURGEONS
15. JACOB'S FACTORY
16. DUBLIN CASTLE

17. CITY HALL
18. TRINITY COLLEGE DUBLIN
19. CUSTOM HOUSE
20. LIBERTY HALL
21. HOPKINS & HOPKINS
22. KELLY'S FORT
23. LOWER ABBEY STREET
24. CLERY'S - IMPERIAL HOTEL

25. NORTH EARL STREET
26. METROPOLE HOTEL
27. HENRY STREET
28. PARNELL MONUMENT
29. GENERAL POST OFFICE
30. O'CONNELL STREET

(GUIDE ONLY — MAP NOT TO SCALE)

4

Introduction

The rebellion which took place in Ireland 83 years ago was arguably the most momentous event in the country's history this century. And yet, in part because of events which followed (which it itself sparked), the Easter Rising is viewed through a clouded lens. Everyone knows a revolt of some sort took place, but to come across someone who knows a bit more detail is rare. To debate why this should be the case would require more space than is available, but there are a couple of reasons which warrant mention.

First is the Civil War which, a mere six years after the Rising, saw former comrades become deadly enemies. With a terrible inevitability, the horror of the Irish Civil War followed the example set by all other civil wars, brother versus brother, father against son. For a long, long time thereafter, trying to look dispassionately at the Easter Rising through the fog of the Civil War was simply impossible. Then (and this is of course a simplification), just as the passions of the Civil War were fading decades later, the new 'Troubles' in the chaos of Northern Ireland were taking their toll on the people of the island, daily creating new chapters in 'modern history' and a new fog through which the history of Ireland in the first quarter of the 20th century was viewed.

The sad result of all this was that, in many circles, to talk of the Rising was considered evidence of holding pro-IRA, pro-terrorism, opinions. And after such a perception has been abroad for a few years, people will begin, naturally, to avoid the subject. This is why, I believe, so little attention has been given to the Rising in recent years. This is why commemorative plaques can disappear from buildings without public comment, and this is why, even today, teachers are confidently telling their nine-year-old charges that the colours of the Irish flag are green, white and gold (they are in fact green, white and orange). Happily, the simple passage of years, along with the changing political climate, means that challenges to this misconception are beginning to be seen, and the time will surely come when the clouds through which we view our own history will disappear.

This book is an attempt to help clear those clouds. By illustrating the locations which were significant during the Easter Rising in 1916 alongside photos of those same locations in 1999, I hope to bring the history of that week to life by making it easier to visualise the events as they happened and where they happened. And by presenting the history of the Rising in the form of short, factual accounts of events, limited to the locations in which they occurred, I hope to capture readers' imaginations and send them towards a further reading of this fascinating subject. After all, history is best appreciated when it jumps from the page and becomes real and identifiable. Who can fail to be moved by the story of the twice daily ceasefires in St Stephen's Green so that the park-keeper could feed the ducks?

The story of the Easter Rising is made up of a large number of smaller stories, of which I've included as many as possible. Some had to be omitted (such as the story of the priests in Westland Row train station on Easter Monday, moving along the platform, listening as the rebels knelt and confessed, still holding their rifles), but others somehow managed to include themselves …

Many of the most moving stories are told by the photographs taken at the time — pictures of earnest-looking men in uniform, barefoot children queueing for food, buildings shattered, bombed, burned and ruined. Thankfully many of the same buildings survive today and if anyone takes the time to look, scars and pockmarks remain to be seen. Photographs were taken at the time, some to be sold as postcards and in souvenir books, some for their newsworthiness, and some out of ordinary curiosity. Many of the pictures reproduced here haven't been in print since 1916 and it's appropriate to pay tribute to the photographers (mainly anonymous) who took them, whatever their motives. Some are in poor condition but I make no apology for their quality, since their historic importance makes them invaluable whatever their condition and it is for the same reason that I have tried to include as many photographs as possible.

One Volunteer actually had a camera with him in the GPO, but his duties meant that he had to put it aside and so we can only speculate about the pictures which might otherwise have been taken. Of course, like the photos that were never taken, there are many stories which will never be told. History is written not only by the winners, but perhaps more importantly, by the survivors. The majority of the men and women who lived through Easter Week never committed their experiences to paper, nor had their memories tapped into by interviewers. And now, in 1999, is there anybody left who remembers the Rising from first-hand experience? Any survivors who took part? It seems not. Volunteer Tommy Keenan was with the rebel garrison in the Stephen's Green area — he was 12 when he sneaked from home to join the fight, so if he was alive today, he would be 95. The stories that were untold will remain so. But there are accounts existing which, although written down, have never been published, and there are also oral histories passed on and still remembered — I would appeal to anyone with such testimonies in their possession or their memory to do whatever they can to make them publicly available.

The fact is that in a matter of months from now, the Easter Rising will be viewed through a new lens — along with everything else that happened in the entire 20th century, it will become something that happened 'last century'. Inevitably, people's perception of this century's events will alter simply because of the change in date — it remains to be seen what form the new perception of the Rising will take. Hopefully its removal to 'last century' won't mean that its importance is diminished in the public eye — and to that end, it would be fitting, I believe, for a new series of plaques to be erected, not just at the locations mentioned in this book, but at all the locations (in and outside of Dublin) that saw history being made in Easter Week, 1916.

Mick O'Farrell, Dublin, March 1999

The Easter Rising, day by day

Apart from some small actions, the 1916 Rising in Dublin lasted seven days, from Easter Monday to the following Sunday. Therefore, when the text mentions 'Wednesday' or 'Friday', for example, without giving a date, it can be assumed that the day referred to is one of the following:

EASTER MONDAY, APRIL 24, 1916:
Beginning of rebellion. Main body of rebels muster outside Liberty Hall — conflicting orders result in a turnout much smaller than hoped for. From about midday on, the following locations are occupied by rebels:
• GPO and other buildings in O'Connell Street area;
• Four Courts, Mendicity Institution;
• St Stephen's Green, College of Surgeons;
• Boland's bakery and surrounding area, including Mount Street Bridge and nearby houses;
• City Hall and several buildings overlooking Dublin Castle;
• Jacob's biscuit factory, Davy's pub by Portobello Bridge;
• South Dublin Union and James's Street area;
• Magazine Fort in Phoenix Park.

Proclamation of Republic read by Pearse outside GPO. Lancers charge down O'Connell Street. Looting starts. That afternoon, the British counterattacks begin.

TUESDAY, APRIL 25, 1916:
City Hall retaken by military. Shelbourne Hotel occupied by soldiers and machine-gun fire forces rebels to retreat to College of Surgeons. British reinforcements, including artillery, arrive. Martial law proclaimed.

WEDNESDAY, APRIL 26, 1916:
Liberty Hall shelled by *Helga,* backed by field guns. Artillery put into action against buildings on O'Connell Street. Kelly's Fort evacuated. Metropole Hotel occupied by rebels. Troops marching from Dun Laoghaire halted by rebels at Mount Street Bridge. After many hours of intense fighting and terrible casualties, the military gain control of the area. Clanwilliam House burns to the ground. Mendicity Institution retaken by British.

THURSDAY, APRIL 27, 1916:
Military shelling of O'Connell Street intensifies. Fires on O'Connell Street begin to rage out of control. Hopkins & Hopkins and Imperial Hotel evacuated because of inferno.

FRIDAY, APRIL 28, 1916:
General Sir John Maxwell arrives in Dublin. Metropole Hotel evacuated. Rebels evacuate GPO. New HQ established in Moore Street.

SATURDAY, APRIL 29, 1916:
Non-combatants murdered in North King Street. Rebel leaders in Moore Street decide to surrender. Four Courts garrison surrenders.

SUNDAY, APRIL 30, 1916:
Rebels in remaining outposts surrender — College of Surgeons; Boland's; Jacob's; South Dublin Union. Deportation of prisoners.

WEDNESDAY, MAY 3 - FRIDAY MAY 12:
Fifteen rebels, including the seven signatories of the Proclamation of the Republic, are executed by firing squad.

Carisbrook House, above, and its replacement.
Note the bullet-holed windows and the soldiers on the steps of the house.

Carisbrook House

Location: Corner of Pembroke Road and Northumberland Road

Map No. 1

This 'imposing residence' lay along the route into the city centre taken by a section of the Sherwood Foresters regiment on Wednesday morning.

British troops had been arriving at Dun Laoghaire from Tuesday night onwards. Many thought they were being shipped to France, some even greeting Dubliners with a 'bonjour'. They set off from Dun Laoghaire at around 10 o'clock on Wednesday morning and at first were greeted by residents along the way offering pots of tea, sandwiches and fruit — 'Thank God you've come,' seemed to be the general greeting.

At about midday, the column of men rested near Carisbrook House. Up until then, they had moved with increasing wariness — the closer they got to the city, the more they expected to be ambushed at any time. But now they took their ease, 'smoking, eating fruit and chatting with civilians who gathered round'.

Their rest was a short one, however, as all of a sudden, several volleys of sniper fire shattered the calm. Many of the soldiers were raw recruits and had never been under fire before, but by all accounts they reacted coolly and dispersed. Thinking Carisbrook House was the source of the gunshots, the soldiers took cover in doorways and behind walls and fired on the house and its gardens, smashing all the front windows and peppering the brickwork.

sniper fire shattered the calm

In fact, no rebels were inside — it had been occupied by rebels on Monday, but was abandoned very shortly afterward.

The rebel company involved in this attack were the Dun Laoghaire-Blackrock contingent, whose original orders called for the holding of the railway station and landing area at Dun Laoghaire pier. However, given the general confusion about the mobilisation that Monday morning, so few Dun Laoghaire-Blackrock Volunteers turned out that the contingent decided to join up with their comrades in the Ringsend area.

Meanwhile there were still some Volunteer snipers in the vicinity of Carisbrook House and they fired 'several volleys of revolver shots' at the soldiers, before withdrawing. Another account says that a few members of the Blackrock Company of Volunteers were 'lurking' in the garden when the soldiers started firing, but they quickly got away.

Carisbrook House was soon occupied by a small number of British soldiers, the rest regrouped and marched on towards 25 Northumberland Road, Mount Street Bridge, and Clanwilliam House — towards an engagement which would be 'the most famous struggle of the whole insurrection.' [TR]

No. 25 Northumberland Road. Note the shattered windows.

25 Northumberland Road

Location: Corner of Northumberland Road and Haddington Road

Map No. 2

Chosen by the rebels for its excellent position commanding the approach from Dun Laoghaire to the city via Mount Street Bridge, No. 25 Northumberland Road was occupied by Lieutenant Michael Malone and Section-Commander James Grace on Easter Monday. Two younger rebels, Rowe and Byrne, were with them, but were sent home the next day by Malone, who said: 'They're not even 16 yet, and the chances are they'll lose their lives if they stay on in this house.'

The owners, being sympathetic to the rebels' cause, had been warned in advance that their house might be occupied and so had left the premises, having first sent their servants away for the holidays.

Around midday on Wednesday, a dispatch was delivered to No. 25 warning that British troops had landed at Dun Laoghaire and were marching on the city. Shortly afterward, those troops appeared on the road leading directly to where Malone and Grace lay in wait.

Ten British soldiers fell at the first volley from No. 25 — five hours of fierce fighting had begun. The surprised British took some moments to realise where the shots were coming from, since they hadn't been expecting resistance until they were closer to Mount Street Bridge. Then suddenly, taking advantage of a gap in the firing from the house, two British officers drew their swords, yelled 'Charge!' and led an assault on the house.

That was the signal for the rebels in nearby Clanwilliam House to fire on the troops — seven more soldiers fell. In Clanwilliam House, the defenders could see firing coming from No. 25; 'Good old Mick! That's the stuff!' yelled George Reynolds, officer-in-charge in Clanwilliam House (see page 19).

A Lee-Enfield rifle — the main weapon of the British Army, it was much sought-after by the rebels in preference to their other antiquated weapons, but was in very short supply

rebel bullets were striking the bell

The British troops were confused by firing which seemed to come from several points simultaneously, and at one point, an officer led his men out from the cover they had sought, into Haddington Road — Malone, with his Mauser automatic pistol at the bathroom window, opened fire and did terrible damage to their ranks.

Meanwhile, rifle and machine-gun fire was being directed into the house from the bell tower of St Mary's Church on Haddington Road. But the rebels returned fire. A civilian medic climbed the tower to help a soldier who had three bullets in his arm and shoulder, and as he tended him, rebel bullets were striking the bell just over his head.

Soon a supply of grenades arrived from the Elm Park Bombing School of Instruction and these were put into immediate service. Again and again, wave after wave of British troops attacked and bombed No. 25 where, despite their continuous devastating firing, Malone and Grace were slowly but surely hemmed in.

Several local residents became casualties, including one incident when a woman was killed and her daughter wounded, both by the same bullet.

Meanwhile bombs and bullets poured into No. 25 (one bomb through a back window caused a huge explosion when it

The plaque on the front wall of No. 25 Northumberland Road. Malone's body was buried in the front garden in full uniform with a handkerchief covering his face

slowly but surely hemmed in

landed among 500 rounds of ammunition). Bullets raked the stairs, bullets came through almost every window and grenades caused constant explosions. Malone and Grace waited to fight it out with rifle and fixed bayonets.

Finally the house was successfully rushed by the troops and Malone was shot dead, 'as he coolly came down the stairs to meet them, his pipe in his mouth.' [PA] Malone's body, in full uniform, was buried in the garden.

Meanwhile, Grace escaped into the kitchen where he cooled his pistol barrel under a tap before hiding behind the cooker. The soldiers failed to find him in a search, so he waited several hours before climbing into another garden, where he hid in a shed, only to be arrested some days later.

Left: Soldiers relaxing while awaiting orders — the location isn't identified, but is possibly Nos. 9 & 11 Northumberland Road, shown above as they are today

No. 25 today — the exterior is largely unchanged. Note how much the saplings in the 1916 picture have grown. Note also the bench — different seat, same location.

Mount Street Bridge, looking towards Clanwilliam House. When soldiers took cover behind the advertising board on the right, the rebels simply peppered the sign with bullets.

Mount Street Bridge

Location: Crossing the Grand Canal, between Northumberland Road and
Mount Street Lower

Map No. 3

The capture of Mount Street Bridge was the goal of the advancing British troops who found themselves halted by terrible fusillades from the surrounding rebel outposts (25 Northumberland Road, the Parochial Hall and the Schoolhouse on one side of the canal, and Clanwilliam House on the other side). Eventually, of course, they achieved their goal, but it required continuous assaults on the bridge, resulting in extremely heavy casualties for the Crown forces. An official dispatch issued by Commander-in-Chief Sir John Maxwell soon after the Rising stated that Mount Street Bridge was 'where our heaviest casualties occurred' — 234 officers and other ranks killed or wounded. The rebel strength in the area numbered 17.

After landing at Dun Laoghaire, the British reinforcements split into three columns to march on the city. Two reached their destination (the Royal Hospital Kilmainham) without incident via Stillorgan-Donnybrook and Ballsbridge-Baggot Street Bridge. The third, thanks to inaccurate intelligence, marched from Ballsbridge to Mount Street Bridge and straight into fierce resistance.

Having bypassed the opposition in No. 25, as well as the Parochial Hall and the Schoolhouse, the troops advanced on the bridge, cautiously at first. Some came from the Baggot Street direction and took what cover they could behind the low wall along the canal bank in Percy Place— however, the haversacks on their backs gave their positions away and the rebels in Clanwilliam House opposite simply blazed away at the khaki humps. (Later in the week, an improvised artillery piece aimed at the rebel garrison in Boland's Bakery, would shatter the windows of houses in Percy Place when it was first fired.)

Looking across Mount Street Bridge from Clanwilliam House.

The houses are on Percy Place — the low wall beside the cars is where soldiers had to crawl to find cover. The spire in the background belongs to the church on Haddington Road, from where a machine-gun and several sharpshooters poured fire into the rebel position in Clanwilliam House.

At the height of the fighting, the rebels in Clanwilliam House looked out on an incredible sight. British troops seemed to be everywhere — in gardens, behind walls, hedges, trees. 'Four great khaki caterpillars pulsated towards them like obscene monsters,' two in the gutters and two against the coping stones along the canal banks. [ER] The rebels poured fire into the troops with devastating effect — as one soldier was killed, another crawled over or around him, only to be halted himself. The entrance to the bridge became a mass of dead and wounded soldiers. Again and again, an officer would step up and lead a few men in a charge over the bridge. And again and again, they would be shot down, falling to join the growing heap of bodies on the bridge. 'After the first few bloody charges of British troops, the bridge was strewn with soldiers, victims of bungled orders, stupidly sacrificed, groaning in agony, … seeking cover behind the dead, … torn bodies, shattered skulls, broiling in a burning haze.' [TR]

The inscription on the back of the monument on Mount Street Bridge, the front of which can be seen on the opposite page

the growing heap of bodies on the bridge

Meanwhile on the city side of the bridge, a crowd of horrified civilians were watching the events. Finally some decided they couldn't simply stand by and, together with some staff from the nearby Sir Patrick Dun's Hospital, sought and were granted permission by the rebels to go onto the bridge and help the wounded. The lull was brief, however — soon a whistle blew and a wave of troops charged the bridge, and were mown down. Every 20 minutes another whistle would blow and another wave of soldiers would charge the bridge, only to be shot down to join the heaps at the bridge's entrance. Then the hospital staff would rush out and rescue as many wounded as possible before the whistle blew again. 'The aprons of the nurses … grew more and more bloodstained.' [ER]

During the final charge over the bridge, a Captain Quibell was forced to play dead half way. 'There were piles of dead and wounded all around me,' he said later. And when the firing from Clanwilliam House seemed to stop (the rebels were out of ammunition), he jumped up and led his men across. The Battle of Mount Street Bridge was over.

Commandant Éamon de Valera

The Mount Street Bridge area fell under the command of de Valera, whose HQ was in Boland's Bakery on Grand Canal Street. With the confusion surrounding rebel mobilisation, far fewer men than expected turned out, so de Valera had to spread his resources very thinly to try and cover all the outposts the Rising's plan called for. That was why there were so few rebels manning the positions around Mount Street Bridge — yet they still managed to hold up an entire British battalion for nearly five hours. However, Boland's Bakery is a very short distance from Clanwilliam House and one of the persistent mysteries of the Rising is why de Valera failed to relieve or reinforce the men who were struggling against such odds.

Mount Street Bridge, looking towards Clanwilliam House. The monument on the left commemorates those who fought and died in the battle

Clanwilliam House soon after its destruction. Note the soldier on guard.

Clanwilliam House

Location: Corner of Clanwilliam Place and Mount Street Lower

Map No. 4

A big, three-storeyed house with commanding views of Mount Street Bridge, the Grand Canal, the Schoolhouse across the canal, and a long stretch of Northumberland Road, Clanwilliam House was politely occupied around midday on Easter Monday by officer-in-charge George Reynolds and a small party of Volunteers. 'May we come in please?' he asked the inhabitants, later instructing his men to act as 'representatives of the Irish Republic ... [not] to behave like hooligans ... and do as little damage as you can.' [ER]

By evening on Wednesday, just two days later, Clanwilliam House was ablaze, having being subjected to sustained attack since about noon that day, when British forces, marching to the city centre after landing at Dun Laoghaire, came under fire as they approached the bridge.

Now an office block, the battle that took place there is best visualised by walking up to the entrance of Clanwilliam House and turning around. The scene on Wednesday April 26th was this: from the tower of St Mary's Church to the right, a machine-gunner and several sharpshooters were pouring bullets into the road outside; the rebels in 25 Northumberland Road were silenced, those in the Parochial Hall were captured; the houses across the canal were occupied by soldiers, more and more of whom were moving towards the bridge in front; and some soldiers had actually made it to the edge of the garden and were throwing bombs into the house.

Nevertheless, despite it all, a tiny body of men managed to hinder the British reinforcements' advance for nine hours. 'Boys, isn't this a great day for Ireland?' roared Volunteer Patrick Doyle as bullets crashed into and around the once-comfortable drawing room of Clanwilliam House. 'Did I ever think I'd live to see a day like this!' he added, just before a bullet entered his head and he went suddenly quiet.

Meanwhile, 17-year-old Jimmy Doyle's rifle overheated and exploded in his face as he fired it into the attacking soldiers — he regained consciousness to find Reynolds wiping blood from his face and giving him a replacement rifle to continue the fight. Eventually the roof was engulfed in flames and the rebels used up the last of their ammunition — their fight was over and it was time to retreat. A basement window less than a foot square was the only way out so they wriggled through into the back garden and over the wall.

a bullet entered his head

British troops finally made it to the front of the house, from where they began battering their way in and throwing bombs through windows (one officer threw a bomb at a first floor window, but it hit the window sill and bounced back before exploding and fatally wounding him).

Of the seven rebel defenders, four escaped death and even, amazingly, capture. Three died within Clanwilliam House — Doyle, Dick Murphy (who was to have been married a week later) and George Reynolds himself.

The intensity of the fire meant that afterwards, apart from a single human leg, 'not a particle of flesh or bone was found' of the three men who died inside Clanwilliam House, which was utterly destroyed in a blaze which lit up streets for miles around. [CA]

And when the battle for Clanwilliam House was over, 'the house next door caught fire and the occupants, Mr and Mrs Mathis, who had crouched in terror in their cellar throughout the battle, sat on deck-chairs in their back garden and watched their home burn down.' [ER]

A Volunteer in full uniform

three died within Clanwilliam House

Another view of Clanwilliam House, clearly showing the bullet marks and the fire damage

Clanwilliam House today is an office block but retains the name

The east side of the Four Courts, showing the results of the artillery's 'clean hits'.
Note the recruitment posters on the wall.

The Four Courts

Location: On the north side of the Liffey, at Inns Quay
Map No. 5

Although it may appear an obvious site for their headquarters, the Four Courts only became the rebels' HQ in that area on Friday. Up until then the HQ was in the Father Matthew Hall further up Church Street.

Nevertheless, the buildings that comprise the Four Courts were occupied immediately after the Rising began — windows were barricaded with whatever came to hand, including chairs, desks and ledgers, and of course, the heavy old law books which were in plentiful supply came in very handy indeed. No permanent damage was done to the legal documents, however. Some bundles fell into the street below and were carried away by local residents — not as loot, apparently, 'but rather as curious souvenirs of the rebellion.' [RH] And in fact, most of these documents were handed back when order was restored.

In the Four Courts, as in their other outposts, the rebels chose to abstain from the alcohol which, in some captured buildings, was plentiful. Too many previous uprisings had suffered from the drunkenness of some participants. A captured British soldier, Captain Brereton, said later: 'The rebels had possession of the restaurant in the Four Courts. It was stocked with wines and spirits and champagne, yet there was no sign of drinking amongst them, and I was informed they were nearly all total abstainers.' [SS] Night fell, and one of the women on duty with the rebels remembered going upstairs where 'we wrapped ourselves in the ermine and sable robes of the judges and we got some sleep.' [CJ]

The military, in the meantime, formed the opinion that the Four Courts itself was a major rebel stronghold, on a par with the GPO. Therefore, they planned to put a military cordon around both these areas. The attempt to encircle the Four Courts involved pushing the cordon down North King Street. General Maxwell wrote: 'We discovered, however, that instead of being outside the rebel area, this line actually cut through it, and

A wide view of the Four Courts, then and now. Although it would appear that nothing much has changed apart from the absence of trams and the presence of trees, the building had a turbulent history in the first quarter of the century.

very desperate fighting occurred before we could complete the cordon.' (This 'desperate fighting' is described in the following sections on North King Street and Church Street.)

On Thursday, a column of soldiers moving from Dublin Castle down to Grattan Bridge came under fire from rebels in the Four Courts (which is at the next bridge upriver) and was scattered. The military's plan couldn't succeed if the rebels commanded Grattan Bridge, so an armoured car was filled with marksmen and sent along the quays. Unharmed by the rebel rifle fire, the car halted opposite the Four Courts and 16 soldiers jumped out and ran into a church graveyard. There they took cover behind the tombstones and began to pour a steady stream of bullets across the Liffey. This definitely lessened the rebel fire directed towards Grattan Bridge, but didn't stop it completely — shots were still being fired at the forces trying to cross the river.

An interesting picture taken inside the Four Courts, showing how the windows were barricaded

they took cover behind the tombstones

Artillery seemed to be a solution, so an armoured car was used to tow a field gun into position across the river from the Four Courts. It was set up on Wood Quay (about where the Civic Offices stand now) and the bombardment began. Several 'clean' hits were scored.

The soldiers soon began to cross the bridge and the armoured cars were then used for loading and unloading sandbags for use as barricades against the rebels. Actually the bags were sacks commandeered from a factory and filled with earth — 'most hovels in the area were so poor that they only had earthen floors, which the troops hacked up.' [ER] It was the beginning of the end for the rebel garrison of the Four Courts.

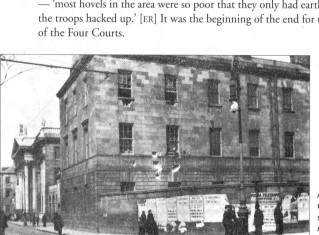

A wider view of the Four Courts, showing the damage sustained. Also visible are more posters seeking recruits for the army.

The east side of the Four Courts today. Note that the surrounding wall has been removed.

Left: The Father Mathew Hall on Church Street, as it looks today. It was here that the rebels set up a Red Cross post during the rebellion.

Right: Commemorative plaque on the Father Mathew Hall on Church Street. Although difficult to spot unless you're looking hard, similar plaques can be seen on the College of Surgeons and on No. 16 Moore Street.

An interesting picture, showing the remains of the rebel barricade at the end of Church Street, where it joins the quays

Church Street

Location: North side of city, running from the Liffey up to North King Street

Map No. 6

Part of the Four Courts area occupied by rebels under Commandant Ned Daly on Easter Monday, Church Street was possibly the first rebel outpost to have a hostile encounter with British forces.

While the rebels were still constructing their barricades (using wooden barrels, empty oil drums, chairs, tables and beds), a troop of British Lancers trotting down the quays suddenly came into view. The mounted soldiers were escorting an ammunition convoy towards their barracks in the Phoenix Park, and had already passed two groups of rebels without incident. But the rebels at the barricade where Church Street joins the quays thought they were about to be attacked and so opened fire. The horses reacted wildly and six or seven Lancers fell to the street, one of them dead.

Panic seemed to overcome the soldiers and the troop split in two — one group regained order and took cover, but a smaller group weren't so lucky. Some surrendered, but two got lost in the side streets. As they galloped wildly around, they fired at rebels ahead of them, but accidentally killed a small girl instead. Then they were fired upon and quickly knocked from their mounts, one of them dead as he fell to the street. This trooper's lance was recovered by the rebels and a tricolour attached to it. It was then carried to the junction of Church Street and North King Street, where it was stuck into a manhole in the middle of the road. Soon a group of rebels stood to attention beside the 'flagpole' and a rifle volley was fired in salute.

Another incident which occurred exactly at the barricade on the quays concerned Lord Dunsany and Army Captain Lindsay, who were driving along on Tuesday, seemingly oblivious to the rebellion all around them. 'Not until a bullet grazed his cheek did Dunsany realise that these disturbances were something more than a mere riot.' [ER]

British Lancers in the Church Street area (The Four Courts Hotel can be seen in the background)

At the barricade, they were halted by a group of rebels, whose captain arrested them. Dunsany was known as a playwright, and, referring to one of his works which was popular at the time, the rebel captain joked that Dunsany wouldn't be entering *The Glittering Gates* just yet. Dunsany congratulated himself on being taken prisoner by literary men. (Later in the week, Dunsany is said to have loaned his razor to some rebels in Jervis Street Hospital, 'so that they might show the cheek of innocence to the British military when they started searching the hospital.')

But unfortunately such pleasantries were short lived. The fighting in the Four Courts area quickly got very dirty — the pressure on defenders and attackers was intense. Church Street was under fire all week from British posts across the river. One sniper in the Bermingham Tower of Dublin Castle was responsible for 53 rebel casualties before he himself was killed on Saturday. Another sniper operated from Christ Church Cathedral's bell-tower, while from the roof of the hospital on Jervis Street a machine-gun spat bullets into the rebel position. On Thursday a man in the Father Mathew Hall in Church Street cracked and began shouting to God to save him from the devils all around — he was given two doses of chloroform to calm him, but it took six men to pin him down in the meantime.

Picture taken from a contemporary postcard — ⬤
caption reads: 'The wreck they made of Church Stre

a machine-gun spat bullets

Towards the end of the week, the military in the area decided to emulate the rebels' tactics and began to break into houses and tunnel from one to the other, all the time getting closer to the rebel positions in Church Street. At one stage in the early hours of Saturday morning, the attackers and defenders were opposite one another on each side of the street, fighting in pitch blackness. 'The sound of crashing timber, the shouted commands of the officers … the scream of bullets resounded continuously. Stabs of flame came from rifles and machine-guns …' [CA]

Now the pressure on the British forces was evident — an impatient colonel refused to wait until the tunnelling was complete. In 12 hours his men had advanced barely 200 yards, on top of which, the rebels were now singing and cheering in between the volleys fired at them. Enough was enough — the soldiers were ordered to charge with fixed bayonets. Unfortunately they ran straight into a wall of bullets fired from several directions — 'It was a terrible slaughter,' recalled rebel Volunteer Frank Shouldice.

The intense fighting continued for hours more, the entire battleground covering just 50 yards at one stage, but eventually news came through of the rebel surrender at headquarters and another episode of the Rising came to an end.

Church Street today – the church in the background is on Thomas Street.

29

Wreckage in the North King Street area

North King Street

Location: North city, parallel to river, intersected by Church Street

Map No. 7

Like Church Street, North King Street formed an important part of the Four Courts area held by the rebel forces during Easter Week. And it was in the middle of the junction of those two streets that a tricolour, attached to a dead British trooper's lance, flew throughout the week.

A pub at that junction quickly became a strong point and gained the nickname 'Reilly's Fort'. At one stage in the battle which raged in the area, British forces, under cover of an armoured car, took up a position behind a barricade opposite the pub. However 'they were met with such a withering fire from the defenders that they retreated in confusion leaving some dead behind.' [DFS] The rebels' firing had been so intense that several of their rifles were put out of action, so they ran out into the road and carried away the rifles left behind by the military.

During another attack, an armoured car drove up North King Street and stopped — 15 soldiers jumped out and 'proceeded to fire into every house along North King Street.' [CA] However, intense rebel fire poured on them from several directions, and their casualties mounted. One soldier tried to break into a house for cover, but as he pounded on the door with the butt of his rifle, it went off and killed a comrade.

After 16 hours of continuous heavy fighting, the rebels in Reilly's were almost out of ammunition. Their only option was to abandon the post and so they dashed out under fire, across North King Street and down into Church Street — amazingly, no-one was injured.

But the almost unbearable strain of the ferocious battle was mounting. British casualties were unacceptably high and their gains were virtually nil. Consequently,

An armoured car used by the military during the Rising. Several armoured cars were constructed in a hurry, some (like this example) using boilers from Guinness's Brewery and the Inchicore Railway Works. Holes were cut in the sides for rifles, with false holes painted alongside the real ones to try and confuse the rebels. Up to 18 men could be transported inside. The cars generally proved ineffective in an assault role, but were very useful for the safe transport and delivery of men and materials under fire. A rebel on the roof of the GPO recalled an armoured car driving down O'Connell Street. He fired repeatedly at the driver's slit until he heard no ricochet, which meant the bullet had gone in. The car ground to a halt. [ER]

it was decided to adopt the rebel tactics of entering houses and tunnelling from building to building. So at two o'clock on Saturday morning, the operation began — an armoured car stopped near No. 172 North King Street and soldiers, armed with crowbars and pickaxes, jumped out and forced their way in.

But by now, for some British soldiers, the pressure had gone past breaking point and they took out their frustration on the non-combatant inhabitants of North King Street.

Military Commander-in-Chief General Sir John Maxwell stated after the rebellion was quashed: 'Possibly unfortunate incidents, which we should regret now, may have occurred. It did not, perhaps, always follow that where shots were fired from a particular house the inmates were always necessarily aware of it or guilty, but how were the soldiers to discriminate? They saw their comrades killed beside them by hidden and treacherous assailants, and it is even possible that under the horrors of this peculiar attack some of them "saw red".'

Nevertheless, the outcome of some soldiers 'seeing red' was devastating for the locals. In No. 170 North King Street, three men were shot — one woman described what appeared to be bayonet wounds on her husband's body, 'several great gashes about the neck and head.' In No. 172, two men were shot — a woman stated that she 'saw soldiers playing cards on a rug thrown over my husband's dead body.' In No. 174, two men were shot — one dying man asked his wife to fetch the soldiers back to finish him off. In No. 27, four men were killed — a soldier was heard to say: 'The little man made a great struggle for his life … but we got him.' [DN]

Commandant Ned Daly

Other allegations of murder in the area were made, but stories of the massacres remained just that — stories, until, on May 10th, the bodies of a further two civilians were unearthed in the cellar of No. 177, where soldiers had hastily buried them 12 inches below the surface. Then an official investigation had to be carried out (the verdict of which was an indictment of the military's behaviour) and 'The Massacres of North King Street' quickly became part of the history of the Four Courts area during Easter Week 1916.

Looking west along North King Street. In the background, where the dark building is, is the junction with Church Street. Behind the wall in the foreground is the approximate location of No. 177 North King Street.

The Mendicity Institution (photograph taken in the 40s or 50s)

Picture courtesy Old Dublin Society

34

The Mendicity Institution

Location: Usher's Island, on south bank of the Liffey
Map No. 8

The Mendicity Institution was at one time the very fine Moira House, with handsome gardens and beautiful rooms, but by 1916 it had been taken over by the Association for the Suppression of Mendicancy, and twice a day, the poor and needy could get meals there.

Its location on the river bank across from the Four Courts, combined with its solidity, meant that on Easter Monday rebel leader James Connolly sent Captain Seán Heuston and a small body of men to occupy the Institution. Their orders were to delay any troops moving towards the Four Courts, so that the rebel garrison there would have sufficient time to get established.

Heuston and his men were expected to hold out for three or four hours. They entered the Mendicity at noon on Monday — they surrendered on Wednesday, nearly 50 hours later.

Their action started an hour after the occupation. By then, the building had been fortified and barricaded when lookouts saw a column of British soldiers marching four-deep out of Collins Barracks across the river. The soldiers crossed the river and marched along the south quays to pass the Mendicity, but they hadn't reckoned on it being held by rebels. The Volunteers opened fire on the soldiers, pouring volley after volley down into the street. The soldiers panicked and began a confused dash for what cover they could find.

Captain Seán Heuston

Within a short time British soldiers flooded the area — the Mendicity's position proved a serious threat to the authorities' strategy for quashing the rebellion. The siege began in earnest.

By Tuesday, the rebels in the Mendicity numbered somewhere around 25. Closing in around them was a force of British soldiers numbering about 350. Rifle and machine-gun fire hammered the Institution's walls relentlessly, but things quietened on Tuesday night. The lull was an ominous one, however — in fact it meant that the soldiers outside were creeping closer and closing any gaps in their surrounding of the building.

The situation for the rebels was now desperate — having been expected to hold out for only a few hours, the garrison was now dangerously low on ammunition and food supplies had run out.

On Wednesday morning, the British soldiers were all around, practically at the Institution's walls. One member of the rebel garrison remembered firing at a soldier only 20 feet away. [CA]

By noon, soldiers were indeed at the walls, from where they began to throw grenades into the building. Against this new threat, the rebels used the only defence they had — they tried to catch the incoming grenades and throw them back. But the grenades wouldn't stop coming. Two rebels were severely wounded when a grenade exploded as they were trying to throw it back out a window. Another Volunteer was killed.

The two wounded men were in danger of dying on the floor of the Institution and their agony, as well as the sheer desperation of their circumstances, persuaded the rebels that the time had come to surrender. With a white flag at their head, the garrison filed out into the yard, but while they were giving themselves up, a shot rang out and one of them dropped dead — killed by a British sniper firing from Thomas Street to the south. It was never discovered whether the shooter was aware that the rebels had surrendered or not.

A nun distributing aid to children — food quickly beca *scarce during the rebellion and the Mendicity Institution* *closed to the poor throughout Easter W*

the grenades wouldn't stop coming

In any case, the rebels' ordeal didn't end with their surrender. One rebel survivor remembered: 'The British were infuriated when they saw the pygmy force that had given them such a stiff battle and caused them so many casualties. They screamed at us, cursed us, manhandled us ... We were forced to march to Collins Barracks with our hands up, held behind our heads. In the barracks we were lined up on the parade ground. Here we were attacked by British soldiers, kicked, beaten, spat upon.' [LW]

British casualties in the siege were over 100, against the rebel garrison's four, and, apart from one 40-year-old, the rebels ranged in age from 18 to Heuston's 25 years. (The nearby Heuston railway station is named after Captain Heuston.)

A column of soldiers moves down Wood Quay

The Royal Hospital Kilmainham was built in the late 1680s for 'ancie[nt] and maimed officers and soldiers'. When the picture above was taken, t[he] Great Hall housed a huge collection of arms and armour, some of [it] dating back to the 16th century. During the rebellion, when Britis[h] reinforcements were shipped to Dublin in strength, the Royal Hospital we[re] used as a makeshift barracks, officers sleeping on the floor of the chap[el] ('we dossed down in front of the altar') and other ranks in the Great Ho[use].

However, by 1922 the Hospital had lost its purpose and the Great H[all] had lost its collection (below). The building was handed over [to] the Free State and the arms and armour were transferre[d] to various armouries in Englan[d]

Royal Hospital Kilmainham

Location: Military Road, Kilmainham
Map No. 9

In 1916 the Royal Hospital Kilmainham housed the British military headquarters in Ireland, and was home to the army's Commander-in-Chief, Ireland. When, on the Wednesday of Easter Week, General Sir John Maxwell was appointed to this position, it was to here that he went on his arrival in Dublin on Friday morning. But the Royal Hospital also played an active role in the rebellion.

One of the positions occupied by the rebels that week was the South Dublin Union, strategically important because of its position near not only the Royal Hospital, but also two barracks, and the main Dublin railway station. The Union, now the site of St James's Hospital, was a huge area of buildings and open fields. With halls, wards, sheds, dormitories, streets, courtyards and two churches, it was a complex bigger than a lot of Irish towns at the time. Its walls also enclosed about 52 acres of fields and lawns. And housed within this sprawl were 3,282 inmates.

With the number of men in his command, rebel Commandant Eamonn Ceannt couldn't possibly have held the entire area securely. However, he spread  his few men as best he could throughout the buildings and in positions covering entrances and boundary walls. One of these rebel positions, as it happened, was barely 300 yards from the Royal Hospital. And so, as fast as possible, the roof and the 60 or so windows of the Royal Hospital which overlook the South Dublin Union were manned by British riflemen and machine-gunners, and the rebel position was constantly sprayed and sniped at from then on.

*Commandant
Eamonn Ceannt*

At one stage on Tuesday, the rebels in the South Dublin Union got together a home-made flag — 'an ordinary window blind with a harp painted in green' — attached it to a pike and raised it from an upstairs window in the Nurses' Home. Then the band of rebels stood to attention and sang *A Nation Once Again*. 'The military reacted at once. From their hard-won positions within the Union, and from the roof of the Royal Hospital … they opened heavy fire. The flag was not damaged. But a woman sitting reading a book in her home in James's Street, and a holidaymaker from Belfast, walking along the South Circular Road, were both shot dead.' [ER]

When the Rising was over, the Commandant Secretary of the Royal Hospital wrote a letter in which he noted: 'No. 2317 Sergt. W. Austin brought a flag in from the South Dublin Union and Sir John Maxwell said it was to be hung up in the Great Hall next to the Instrument of Torture for Rebels. This will be done in due course.' The Secretary added: 'The pike to which the flag was attached was quite new and looks as if the rebels meant business with it.' [KG]

PHENIX PARK, DUBLIN. (ISLAND BRIDGE ENTRANCE.)

The Islandbridge entrance to the Phoenix Park, through which the Officer-in-Charge's son ran to try and raise the alarm

Magazine Fort, Phoenix Park

Location: Islandbridge Gate, southern side of Phoenix Park

Map No. 10

Surprising as it may seem, one of the most important things which Volunteer Garry Holohan had to do on Easter Monday morning was to buy a football…

He was one of the party of rebels who had been assigned the task of blowing up the Magazine Fort inside the Islandbridge Gate of the Phoenix Park. The British military used the Fort as a store for arms, ammunition and high explosives, and the rebel plan was that the noise of the explosion would be loud enough to serve as an aural signal to their comrades throughout the city that the Rising was to begin.

An area known as the Fifteen Acres, near the Fort, was regularly used by Dubliners as a football ground, and, especially on a bank holiday, one group of men kicking a ball about would blend right in with all the other groups. And so the rebels arrived from several directions and met up on the football ground — Holohan had his football, bought in a shop on Ormond Quay along the way.

The rebels began their 'game'. For only a couple of minutes, the ball was kicked around, and then it was 'accidentally' kicked over to land near the Fort's sentry. A number of rebels gathered round the sentry, with the supposed purpose of retrieving their ball — the soldier was quickly overpowered, and the rebels were inside.

Holohan had his football

Six months previously, another Volunteer, Paddy Daly, had gotten himself a job with a building firm which was hired to carry out repairs inside the Fort, so by the time the raid came, he was very familiar with the Fort's layout and the comings and goings of the guards. There was a main store where the high explosives were kept, and another store for small arms and ammunition — Daly also knew precisely where the keys to these stores were kept.

The sentry and 10 other soldiers were taken prisoner, but one soldier, when he put up a defence, was shot twice and died later. The Fort Commander was in France at the time, but his wife, Mrs Playfair, and three children were in the Fort and also taken prisoner. The designated Officer-in-Charge (OC) of the Fort was also away, having chosen to spend his bank holiday at the Fairyhouse races.

The phone line was cut, and Mrs Playfair and her children were released with a warning that the Fort's stores would be blown up in six minutes. Then Paddy Daly went for the key to the main store — but it wasn't there. The OC had absent-mindedly taken it with him and so, instead of being in the Fort where it belonged, the key to the military's most important arms store in Dublin was in an officer's pocket — at the races.

The rebels had to make do with what they could find in the small-arms store — five bags of gelignite. This was piled up by the wall of the main store with ammunition belts on top, and a fuse was set. In the meantime, rifles and ammunition were being gathered from the stores and taken from the guard. Then the fuse was lit.

Part of the rebels' plan called for these captured weapons to be driven away after the raid and a Volunteer was under orders to commandeer a car and have it waiting with the engine running. The Volunteer had indeed stolen a car, but on the way to the Phoenix Park, had managed to drive it straight into a lamppost. So the vehicle which waited for the captured arms was a jaunting car with a frightened driver. Nevertheless, the guns were piled on and the horse trotted off with a few rebels also on board.

A lump of melted cartridges and clips recovered from the Magazine Fort after the Rising

a jaunting car with a frightened driver

As they left the Fort behind, someone noticed a boy running out through the Islandbridge gate — it was Mrs Playfair's oldest son. The risk of the boy raising the alarm was too great and so Volunteer Holohan took off after him on a bicycle. The boy had a good head start, but Holohan was gaining all the time. Then young Playfair ran to a row of houses and up to the door of the first one. Holohan jumped from the bicycle, drew his pistol and aimed. 'Holohan saw a desperate face glance back at him … It was over in an instant … [he] fired three times.' [ER] The youth was fatally wounded.

Almost simultaneously, the gelignite in the Fort exploded. The rebels had hoped that the explosion might blow through the wall of the main store and set off the whole dump, but it didn't happen. 'Perhaps this was fortunate,' remembered one of the rebels later, 'as we should never have been able to get out of the place in time.' [CA]

The Magazine Fort as it looks today

The Islandbridge entrance today

PORTOBELLO BRIDGE AND HOSPITAL, DUBLIN.

Portobello Bridge — Davy's pub is on the right

44

Portobello Bridge

Location: Crosses the Grand Canal at Rathmines Road
Map No. 11

In April 1916, the pub beside the Portobello Bridge was owned by a man called Davy, who had a reputation for being hard on his staff — he was known as the 'ould blackguard'. At the time, one of the men working for Davy went by the name of James Joyce.

Joyce was 35 and his normal working week saw him in the cellar of Davy's pub, seven days a week, up to 12 hours a day. However, Joyce was also a member of the Irish Citizen Army (one of the two organisations whose men and women participated in the Rising) but Davy refused to allow him time off on Sundays to parade with his comrades. Indeed Davy had warned Joyce that if he took a Sunday off he'd be sacked.

But the pub's location on the Portobello Bridge happened to make it important to the rebels' plans for the Rising. From Davy's, they could halt any military advance from Portobello (now Cathal Brugha) Barracks towards St Stephen's Green. The occupation would be a short one, but it would be long enough to allow the Stephen's Green garrison sufficient time to get established.

So when midday arrived on that Easter Monday, James Joyce was a happy man — he was assigned to the party of rebels ordered to occupy Davy's pub under Sergeant Joseph Doyle and, with his knowledge of the premises, he was allowed to lead the attack.

firing steadily into the pub

Joyce kicked the door in and entered, walking straight over to where Davy was pulling a pint. 'I'm giving you a week's notice, Joyce!' the 'ould blackguard' shouted, banging the counter. Davy, in his surprise at seeing Joyce, must have failed to notice the rifles he and his comrades carried. His surprise, however, must surely have been nothing compared to Joyce's pleasure…

'And I'm giving you five minutes, Mister Davy!' roared Joyce in reply, before lifting his gun and shooting at the shelves — glass bottles smashed as Davy dived for cover. [ER]

Very soon afterwards, the rebels were in action against the military. James Connolly's orders to Doyle were plain: 'Don't fire on the military until you see the whites of their eyes!' The barracks was close by, and so it wasn't long before soldiers on their way to defend Dublin Castle were attacking Davy's in earnest — the obstacle had to be removed.

When Liam Ó Briain (a rebel on his way to join another outpost) arrived at Portobello Bridge in the afternoon, British soldiers were lined up all along the bank opposite Davy's, firing steadily into the pub. They formed two perfect lines as if under inspection — in front, soldiers fired from a lying position, while behind, a second row were kneeling as they fired. Their commanding officer stood behind, the back of his tunic ripped by a bullet. Meanwhile on the bridge, more soldiers manhandled a machine-gun into position and started a hail of bullets streaming towards the building. All the while, crowds of people on Rathmines Road were cheering and shouting and had to be forced back by the police.

But Ó Briain noticed that no firing was returned by the rebels within. The British officer aimed his revolver at him and barked: 'Go back, you!'

Soon, an officer ordered an assault on Davy's — soldiers rushed the pub and, using their rifle butts, smashed the windows and 'rushed into the house, which they searched from garret to cellar, only to find … that the rebels had made good their escape.' [RH]

Another contemporary account says: 'A search of the premises was disappointing to the soldiers; the facilities to escape in many directions had been fully availed of.' [SR]

By the time the military stormed the building, the rebels in St Stephen's Green had been given the time they needed. The men in Davy's had done their job and — exactly as according to plan — they had then left their outpost to join the rebel strongpoints. James Connolly had told Joyce that when the time came for them to evacuate, he was to 'get them out of that pub the quickest and safest way you know.'

The modes of transport have changed dramatically over 80 years, but, apart from its name, Davy's pub is remarkably unchanged

Dunshelm Bridge Anglos. The hospital is now a college and Dunsen Lodge is now the Dunshelm Park

47

St Stephen's Green, looking towards the Shelbourne Hotel

St Stephen's Green

Location: South city
Map No. 12

Intersecting so many major routes from the south of the city into the centre, St Stephen's Green was an important location in the rebels' plans for Easter Week. British reinforcements marching into the heart of Dublin would inevitably have to pass through or by the Green.

Unfortunately for the rebels, circumstances dictated that far fewer numbers turned out than were planned for. Nevertheless, on Easter Monday morning, Volunteers and members of the Irish Citizen Army marched up Grafton Street and entered the Park. Civilians were ordered to leave, off-duty soldiers were taken prisoner, gates were shut and barricaded. Then, in an echo of the Great War being fought at that moment in France, the rebels started digging trenches.

The main gate, under the arch at the Grafton Street end, was closed and almost immediately approached by a Royal Irish Constable called Michael Lahiff. He was told to go away and, having refused, he was shot dead. Several accounts put Countess Markievicz at the gate, shooting her Mauser rifle-pistol (one quotes her as shouting: 'I shot him! I shot him!' [ER]). Certainly the Countess and her Mauser were kept busy at other times, including trying to silence machine-guns in the Shelbourne or, in her own words: 'tackling any sniper who was particularly objectionable'. Her comrades remembered her standing firm and refusing to take cover as bullets whipped the grass and trees around her.

I shot him! I shot him!

...t of the ...ntess in ...ephen's Green

CONSTANCE
MARKIEVICZ

MAJOR
IRISH CITIZEN ARMY
1916

Vehicles going by were stopped by rebels with revolvers and fixed bayonets and their drivers ordered to place them in barricades which were put up across the roads around the Green. One vehicle was a 'splendid motor-car' in which was being driven 'a dignitary of the Catholic Church.' Occasionally a driver would be slow to obey and a bullet would be fired into a tyre as persuasion. Some people tried to recover items from the barricades, but were fired on — one man ignored repeated warnings and was shot dead. At the corner of Merrion Row (about where the double-arch sculpture stands now) a horse lay dead in a pool of blood and remained there for days.

Because Stephen's Green is so open, rebel Commandant Michael Mallin ordered that a number of houses and buildings on the perimeter be occupied to secure their positions. Amongst these was the College of Surgeons near Grafton Street (see page 57). However, there simply weren't enough men to hold all the buildings necessary, and one which was left unoccupied was the Shelbourne Hotel (see page 53).

This omission became most obvious at four o'clock the next morning, when machine-gun bullets began to pour into the Green from the windows and roof of the Shelbourne — the laboriously-dug trenches provided scant protection and rebels soon began to drop around the Green. One young rebel ran for the railings and had almost cleared them when an arc of bullets hit him, knocking him to the ground. His crawling attracted a second sweep of machine-gun fire, and this time, he was stopped for good. Machine-gun fire continued to strafe the park, and whenever the dead youth's body was hit, the gunners — believing he was still alive — fired into the corpse again and again.

Mallin ordered the evacuation of the Green and, in groups of twos and threes, the rebels dodged bullets and dashed across to the College of Surgeons. One man was shot dead.

However, some of the Green's occupants had an easier time of it — although regularly scattered by the bursts of machine-gun fire coming from the Shelbourne, the Green's duck population at least didn't want for food. Twice a day, park-keeper James Kearney would leave his cottage in one corner of the Green to feed the ducks — and twice a day the firing from all sides would stop to allow the ducks to be fed.

Monument to the Fianna (boy scout movement) in the Green

bullets began to pour into the Green

A barricade of motor-cars on the south side of the Green

The main entrance to St Stephen's Green

Ducks on calmer waters in St Stephen's Green. The top of the Shelbourne Hotel is just visible over the treetops in the left background

The imposing façade of the Shelbourne Hotel, as seen from inside St. Stephen's Green

Shelbourne Hotel

Location: North side of St Stephen's Green, corner of Kildare Street
Map No. 13

Since it commanded such excellent fields of fire over St Stephen's Green, the occupation of the Shelbourne Hotel was planned by the rebels from the beginning. But, for a variety of reasons, the mobilisation of the rebel forces on Easter Monday turned out to be much less than planned for. And so, while the Green was being fortified, the Shelbourne was largely left alone — not because it was too heavily defended, but because '50 Volunteers and Citizen Army men who should have taken it were simply not there.' [TR]

The result was catastrophic for the rebels. At two o'clock in the early morning of Tuesday, over a hundred British soldiers were moving up Kildare Street towards the Shelbourne. Captain Carl Elliotson was in charge — he had been ordered to occupy the hotel and 'have a go' at the rebels entrenched in Stephen's Green. Wary of being discovered by their enemy, the soldiers did their best to advance in silence — 'strict orders were issued that the men should advance in the dark on tiptoe.' [TR]

That was the idea. However, the soldiers were all carrying heavy loads, averaging 500 rounds of ammunition each, as well as machine-gun parts, spares and regular equipment. They were also all wearing hobnailed army boots.

rebels awoke to bullets thudding into grass

Elliotson and his men were sure they would be heard but in fact they entered the Shelbourne unchallenged. The hotel was quickly fortified — all entrances were placed under guard, two men were put at every window, and the company's machine-guns were set up on the fourth floor.

Meanwhile, below the hotel windows in Stephen's Green, the rebels got what sleep they could, some in the trenches they'd dug during the day, some in the park's summer house. But their rest was soon to be shattered.

When a distant bell ceased ringing the hour of four, the guns in the windows and on the roof of the Shelbourne Hotel opened fire. From a machine-gunner's point of view, the field of fire over Stephen's Green could hardly be better — the rebels below woke to bullets thudding into grass and whizzing through branches. Their position was simply untenable — finally, and fatally for some, the rebels evacuated the Green for the solid walls of the College of Surgeons on the west side.

Volunteer Margaret Skinnider offered to cycle past the hotel and throw some of their home-made bombs in through the windows — 'Too dangerous,' said Mallin, refusing permission.

All through the rest of Easter Week, the British gunners in the Shelbourne poured fire into the rebel positions across the Green. The pro-Empire *Irish Times* reported that 'the military took up positions in the Shelbourne Hotel … and vigorous sniping of the rebels followed.'

Indeed, snipers featured largely in the tactics of both sides throughout the rebellion. At one stage in the fighting around St Stephen's Green, a British sniper dressed himself as a maid and set to his task from a window in the Shelbourne. For quite some time his disguise was successful and he shot at the rebel positions with impunity. Finally his ruse become apparent and a rebel bullet through the head silenced him.

On another occasion, British soldiers telephoned a shop which was occupied by rebels, and military snipers waited to shoot whoever picked up the phone, which was by a window. The phone rang and a rebel captain stood to answer it — fortunately, he was tackled to the ground by a comrade before he could lift the receiver.

*a rebel
bullet
through
the head
silenced
him*

Countess
Markievicz's
Mauser
rifle-pistol

*The commanding view of St Stephen's Green from the windows of the Shelbourne Hotel.
The portico of the College of Surgeons is clearly visible in the background, to the right.*

The Shelbourne today

The Royal College of Surgeons on St Stephen's Green

Royal College of Surgeons

Location: West side of St Stephen's Green
Map No. 14

Shortly after his forces entered St Stephen's Green on Easter Monday, rebel Commandant Mallin ordered that the College of Surgeons be occupied in order to serve as a reserve post. In fact, holding the Surgeons building hadn't been part of their original plans, but the rebels were very soon to be glad of the protection its walls offered.

Early on Tuesday, with bullets zipping on all sides, the Green was abandoned by the rebels, who were forced to leave several dead comrades 'lying at full length on the ground' behind the railings. During the evacuation, the military machine-guns firing from the Shelbourne Hotel were aimed at rebels on the Surgeons roof. Several bullets found one rebel, Private Michael Doherty.

His comrades on the road below saw Doherty collapse onto the parapet and it looked as though he might fall into the street — his head and arms hung over the front of the building, dripping blood which stained the facade. The machine-gun continued to strafe the rooftop. Captain Joseph Connolly ran as fast as he could across the road, into the College, up and out onto the roof. To the cheers of the rebels below, and by risking his own life, Connolly dragged Doherty to safety.

He had been hit 15 times — a comrade looked at his bloody face and said: 'I'm afraid you're a goner, Mick; may the Lord have mercy on your soul.' However, despite losing an eye and the use of one hand, Doherty survived, only to die in the flu epidemic of 1918.

...mbers of the Irish Citizen Army

...'m afraid you're a ...oner, Mick ...

Meanwhile, one rebel was delighted to be in the thick of things — Tommy Keenan had been ordered home by the rebels on Monday, and his father had locked him in his room. But the youngster got out a window and clambered down a drainpipe so he could return to the fight — Tommy Keenan was 12 years old.

Inside the College, another young rebel got into trouble with his Commandant. The youth had slashed a portrait of Queen Victoria and ripped it from its frame. 'This'll do for leggings,' he said.

When Mallin saw the damage he was enraged at the wanton destruction and shouted: 'If we find the man who did that I'll shoot him!' The boy came up and asked: 'Is it Queen Victoria you're talking about, sir? Here's a bit of her if you want it.' And he helpfully offered a bit of canvas to the Commandant. 'So it was you, you scamp!' roared Mallin, before giving the culprit a clip on the ear.

A severe lack of food quickly became a problem for the rebel garrison and tunnels were bored from building to building in increasingly desperate efforts to find supplies — towards the end of the week, some rebels simply fainted at their posts from hunger and exhaustion.

Occasionally, patrols were sent from the College to deal with snipers — during one sortie, Margaret Skinnider turned to her 17-year-old comrade, only to see him shot dead before her eyes, moments before she herself was shot and seriously wounded. Although she refused to allow herself be taken to hospital, Skinnider survived, but not before overhearing someone say, while she lay in the College of Surgeons: 'That's the death rattle.'

that's the death rattle …

All the while Countess Markievicz's mood remained defiant. Watching the fires of the city centre from the roof of the College, she remarked: 'Think of it — that's not Rome burning, but Dublin!' Then when the rebellion was nearing its end, she wanted to fight to the last man standing, and her main concern was that she 'had no stabbing weapon for close quarters work — I'll have to get a bayonet or sword or something.' Mallin simply remarked: 'My, my, but you're very bloodthirsty!'

When the surrender of the College of Surgeons garrison finally came on Sunday, Markievicz raised her Mauser rifle-pistol and kissed it before formally handing it over. The British officer who took it — Captain Wheeler — then said: 'I can place a motor-car at your disposal, madam.' (As a countess, even a rebel one, Markievicz was several rungs higher up the social ladder than a mere army captain, and Wheeler recognised that fact.)

But Markievicz declined, saying with pride: 'No, I shall march at the head of my men as I am Second-in-Command, and shall share their fate.'

Rebel Commandant Michael Mallin and his Second-in-Command, Countess Markievicz after their surrender

A member of Cumann na mBan, the women's volunteer organisation which featured prominently throughout Easter Week

Throughout the Easter Rising, women played as important a role as their male comrades, although, perhaps because of the social circumstances of the day (and indeed, later days), or perhaps because they were simply fewer in number, there are fewer published accounts of their involvement. One notable exception is The Women of 1916 — see bibliography.

59

Jacob's biscuit factory — Bishop Street is to the left, and Peter Row is to the right

Jacob's Factory

Location: Corner of Bishop Street and Peter Row
Map No. 15

The site where Jacob's Biscuit Factory stood in 1916 is now occupied by the Dublin Institute of Technology — the present building is impressive in size, but the former factory was an even more imposing structure. In the Dublin skyline of the day, the tall buildings and even taller towers provided excellent views over most of the city.

When the rebels arrived to occupy Jacob's at around midday on Easter Monday, they brought axes and hammers to force the main gate in Bishop Street, while at the Peter Row end, a ladder was chained to a lamppost and swung against the windows to open them. While all the crashing and banging of a forced entry was going on, two policemen arrived to remonstrate with what must have looked to them like a band of thieves — six rifles were immediately pointed at them and they were told to mind their own business.

Getting into the factory proved a bit more difficult for any rebels who arrived late. One late arrival was Martin Walton — although a member of the Volunteers, Walton was only 15, so his parents had taken the valves from the wheels of his bicycle to prevent him going into town to join the rebellion. He got away on Tuesday, nevertheless, and went to join his battalion in Jacob's. When he arrived, there was a hostile mob blocking his way, so he shouted up to the windows: 'Let me in, let me in.' But a 'very big tall woman' came at Walton from behind, carrying something very heavy which she lifted and went to hit him with — a rebel in the factory saw her and shot at her. 'I just remember seeing her face and head disappear as she went down like a sack. ... I would have sold my mother and father and the Pope just to get out of that bloody place. But you recover after a few minutes.' [CJ]

Thomas MacDonagh, Commandant in Jacob's, executed after the surrender

rebel snipers were busy

Meanwhile, the rebels stationed in the towers had field glasses through which they spotted, and reported on, British troop movements in the streets far below. Rebel snipers were busy throughout the week, harassing the military advancing to augment the Dublin Castle garrison, as well as picking off soldiers in their barracks in Rathmines, and, indeed, even as far off as St Stephen's Green.

One of the rebel officers wasn't entirely happy about their position, however. Major John MacBride had fought on the Boer side during the Boer War. 'Why don't we fight

A Jacob's lorry on Eden Quay after the Rising

61

them as the Boers did,' he wondered, 'instead of locking ourselves up in a whole lot of buildings?'

One advantage Jacob's had over many of the rebel strongholds was that there was no shortage of foodstuffs, even if they weren't exactly 'suitable for hungry men'. Máire Nic Shiubhlaigh, who was in charge of the women volunteers, noted that: 'There were biscuits in plenty — 'plain and fancy' — mostly fancy — slabs of rich fruit cake, some shortbread, and a few tons of cream crackers.'

Major John MacBride, executed after the surrenc

Small parties of men were sent out by the rebel Commandant Thomas MacDonagh to man outposts or to gather intelligence. One such sortie prematurely attacked the advance guard of a British column which was moving down

a few tons of cream crackers

Camden Street towards Dublin Castle. Seven soldiers were wounded, but the main body, instead of walking straight into a wall of gunfire from the factory itself, took the warning and retreated, before choosing a different route into the city.

Capturing Jacob's posed a dilemma for the military. The entire surrounding area was a mass of small houses which, on the one hand, would have made direct assaults on the factory very costly in terms of men. On the other hand, if artillery were to be used to pound the garrison into submission, the same concentration of houses and buildings would have to be completely razed first, to create effective fields of fire.

In the event, an attack on the rebels in Jacob's was rendered unnecessary, since before the military had to make that decision, another one was made for them. Rebel Commander-in-Chief Pearse surrendered on Saturday and, although disbelieving at first (if Pearse ordered a general surrender after he himself surrendered, then perhaps his orders were invalid since they could have been made under duress), MacDonagh, with tears in his eyes, ordered his men to surrender also.

Some were so despondent at these orders that they smashed their rifles. Eventually the rebel garrison marched out of the factory and surrendered their guns and ammunition. 'All the time a solitary sniper continued firing. We afterwards learned he was one of our own men — located in some high position in Jacob's — who had not heard of the surrender.' [CA] Meanwhile, as the rebels were handing over their weapons, 'the crowd then indulged in looting on an extensive scale, many bags of flour and boxes of biscuits being carried off.'

A side view of Jacob's factory — the front of what is now the DIT is towards the back of the picture

Bayonets at the ready, soldiers stand guard at the gates of Dublin Castle

Dublin Castle

Location: Top of Dame Street, at opposite end to Trinity College Dublin

Map *No. 16*

The main gate to Dublin Castle was where the first fatality of the Easter Rising occurred. Just after noon on Monday, a nurse, on her way into the Castle's hospital (set up for the war), passed the policeman on duty. 'Is it true that the Sinn Feiners are going to take the Castle?' she asked. 'Ah no, miss,' he replied, 'I don't think so.' A couple of minutes later, he fell to the ground, dead.

A small party of rebels led by Seán Connolly had marched up Dame Street and approached the Castle gate, but Constable James O'Brien tried to bar them and was shot in the head. When another policeman approached around a corner, Helena Molony drew her revolver and fired into the air, sending him running. A soldier on duty at the gate fired a shot before running for cover.

While the rest of the guards fled, the rebels rushed into the guardroom and took three soldiers prisoner, before helping themselves to the meal which had been left cooking on the fire. Some rebels stayed at the Castle entrance, while the rest occupied City Hall next door. If Connolly had known that the Castle was guarded at that time by less than 25 soldiers, he might have pressed the attack and captured the entire centre of British administration in Ireland. In fact, though, it's arguable that he wouldn't have, since, due to the conflicting mobilisation orders given over the weekend, the rebels simply didn't have the manpower to take and hold the Castle, even if it was severely undermanned.

Seán Connolly

Instead their plan was to prevent soldiers from entering or leaving the Castle, and to this end, they occupied City Hall and some surrounding buildings, particularly the offices of the *Mail & Express* newspapers on the corner of Cork Hill and Parliament Street.

From these vantage points, the rebels poured a steady stream of bullets at targets within the Castle walls. Their comrades on the roof of Jacob's factory a couple of blocks away also did their best to make life difficult for the soldiers. The result was that the military were convinced that the number of attacking rebels was far greater then it was.

To the authorities, the idea that Dublin Castle — the seat of British government for Ireland, with all that that title represented — could be attacked and threatened by a band of rebels was simply unacceptable. And so as soon as men were available, the task of rooting out the rebels was begun instantly. A sniper started firing from the Bedford clock tower in the Castle almost immediately, and soon after, the clock was put out of action by the rebels' return fire. A Vickers machine-gun was set up by the British as soon as a concealed position with good field of fire was found — soon its bullets were smacking into the walls of City Hall and the Rates Office beside it.

From the Castle, the military launched successive assaults against City Hall and, within half an hour of dawn on Tuesday, the rebel defenders gave up the fight (see page 69).

In the offices of the *Mail & Express*, however, the operation took longer. After a spectacular 15-minute barrage of rifle and machine-gun fire from the Castle, a wave of soldiers rushed out of the Castle gate with fixed bayonets and ran towards the rebel position. Three minutes later another wave ran from the gate. Then another and another. Wave after wave of soldiers were thrown at the entrance to the building, but although they were vastly superior in numbers, the narrowness of the space they were attacking worked against them. One wave would rush the doorway, only to find

British soldiers (these are on guard in Clontarf) with some of the weaponry available to them

run, you young fool, run

themselves blocked by the casualties caused during the previous assault. The noise of the attack grew almost unbearable and the smoke was intense.

One British soldier moving around to the rear of the building, found himself pointing his bayonet at his brother — who was fighting with the rebels. 'Lowering his bayonet, he hissed, "Run, you young fool, run!"' [ER]

Eventually, of course, the sheer weight of numbers decided the outcome and the rebels in the area were beaten. Casualties on both sides were high — a contemporary account spoke of one room where 'the floor, walls, and doors were literally bathed in blood.'

In 1916, Dublin Castle was the seat of the British government for Ireland

City Hall as seen looking down Cork Hill towards Dame Street

City Hall

Location: On Cork Hill, beside Dublin Castle
Map No. 17

This solid and imposing building has an important position overlooking not just Dublin Castle itself, but also the approaches to the Castle. As such, it was occupied as soon as the rebellion began.

Once inside City Hall (using a specially-made key to open the door), the rebels moved quickly to the rooftop, from where they harassed any troop movements below, whether within, or to and from, the Castle.

The rebels were led by Captain Seán Connolly, who was employed in the Motor Tax office in City Hall and therefore was familiar with the building. Connolly was also a talented actor and was to take the lead role in a play by Yeats on Easter Tuesday. However, the Rising intervened and, just after two o'clock on Monday afternoon, Connolly became the rebels' first casualty of the Rising — he was shot dead by a British sniper firing from the clock tower in Dublin Castle.

Before long, the military were attacking City Hall in ever-increasing numbers, machine-gun bullets were spewing from the Castle, breaking windows, splintering wood and raising clouds of plaster and stone dust. At one point two women members of the rebel garrison looked out the window and thought there had been an odd change in the weather — it seemed as if it was hailing outside. They looked again: it was sheets of bullets streaming past the window.

sheets of bullets streaming past the window

A rebel bullet found after the Rising

Meanwhile up on the roof, the rebels also kept up a constant rifle fire. So constant in fact, that barrels overheated and men had to wrap handkerchiefs around their hands to stop them being burned by the metal.

Eventually the military threw 200 troops into the assault on City Hall, against the rebel garrison of around 20. The soldiers would dash out of the Castle gates, onto the street and around to the front entrance of the Hall. Many were caught by heavy rifle fire from the rebels on the roofs of the buildings around City Hall — one charge alone left 20 soldiers lying on the street in front of the Hall before the rest of the wave retreated.

It was now Monday night and, in the darkness, other soldiers entered the Hall through its back windows which they reached by moving unseen through the Castle cellars. To the noise of rifle and machine-gun fire was added the booming explosions of grenades thrown in through the windows. The rebels thought the Hall's dome was going to collapse. The military forced them up to the first floor, but were soon beaten back by rebel volleys.

As those soldiers descended in the darkness, they ran straight into another group of soldiers trying to go up the stairs. Each mistook the other for a party of rebels and opened fire, stabbing and slashing with their bayonets. When the tragic mistake was corrected, the soldiers advanced again and overwhelmed the rebels upstairs.

The remaining rebels on the roof waited for the final assault, sure that they'd soon be killed, but it seemed to be delayed and the shooting below had stopped. By then, many of the rebels' rifle barrels were so hot they were unusable, so a break to allow them to cool was welcomed.

However, as they moved up through the building, the military had been taking prisoners. One rebel, Jenny Shanahan, wasn't in uniform and the soldiers assumed she had been a prisoner of the rebels. 'Are there many of them here?' she was asked. 'There must be hundreds of them still up there on the roof,' was her quick reply.

Plaque outside City H

stabbing and slashing with their bayonets

After the dreadful confusion earlier in the dark, the military decided they were happy to leave the rebels alone and cut off on the roof. There would be plenty of time to deal with them in the morning.

Sure enough, as soon as daylight arrived, machine-gun fire scoured the roof, in preparation for the final attack. Thirty minutes after dawn, the rebels were defeated. Two had been killed, one escaped by climbing into a chimney, and the rest were led away to prison.

A view of the other side of City Hall, looking up Cork Hill. The street directly opposite the entrance is Parliament Street.

A view of Trinity College Dublin from College Green (note the absence of trees)

Trinity College Dublin

Location: South side of city centre
Map No. 18

Trinity College, a large complex of strong-walled buildings with an excellent situation on the south side of O'Connell Bridge, remained in pro-British hands throughout the rebellion. No serious attempt to capture it was made by the rebels, although at the time the GPO was being occupied, the whole of Trinity contained only eight armed men who could have put up any defence (an Officers' Training Corps, OTC, had been established in the College in 1910).

Of course, there was no way the rebel leaders could have known that, and, in any case, because of the confusion surrounding the call to rebellion that Monday morning, the insurgents simply didn't have sufficient men to attempt a takeover of the College.

However, the word went out, and absent members of the OTC were rounded up. 'Stray' British soldiers (some on leave from the front in France) were pressed into service, and by seven that evening, the number of defenders had risen to around 150.

A contemporary account described how Trinity looked that day: 'The great gates of the College were closed and barricaded, the windows filled with sandbags, over which peeped the barrels of the defenders' rifles.' Among the defenders were some Anzac soldiers who were stationed on the roof — their accuracy with their rifles would prove a severe thorn in the rebels' side throughout the week. Very soon after the order to fire at will was given, the Anzacs fired four shots at some rebels who were cycling by. One was killed outright. 'It was wonderful shooting,' wrote a member of the OTC, adding, 'three [bullets] found their mark in the head of the unfortunate victim.'

The body lay in an empty room for three days before being buried temporarily in College Park. (Two British soldiers were also buried in the College grounds later in the week.) Nevertheless, some students did their best to continue college life as if nothing untoward was happening in the city outside — nearly 20 students turned up on Tuesday for an exam. Some even returned on Wednesday for

The gates of TCD under guard

another exam, despite the presence in the College at that time of hundreds of British troops (not to mention the artillery shelling, the sniping and the constant machine-gun firing going on outside). One student wrote of seeing a dead soldier carried past her on a stretcher. Finally the College authorities suspended the rest of the examinations. [TI]

An officer in the uniform of Trinity's OTC

Meanwhile, from a corner of the College's roof, a sniper could get a clear view down as far as the GPO on O'Connell Street and it was from there that one military sniper demonstrated his marksmanship. Communications between rebel headquarters in the GPO and Commandant Brennan-Whitmore's outpost across O'Connell Street had been established by means of a loop

the college became a fortress

of string, attached to which was a tin can. Dispatches would be put in the can and pulled back and forth across the street. Not long after being set up, the can was pulled in and found to have a bullet hole clean through it. 'Did I get it?' whooped a delighted Australian soldier when he met Brennan-Whitmore during the latter's detention after the Rising.

Meanwhile the importance of Trinity's location wasn't lost on the British military — it was crucial to General Lowe's strategy to crush the rebellion. The College became a fortress and soon hosted 4,000 troops, including infantry, artillery and cavalry. So many horses and men were milling about, that Trinity had 'the appearance of a vast open-air stable or horse fair.' From here the General pushed a cordon out into the city centre and gradually the rebel outposts were isolated from their leaders at the GPO headquarters.

And it was through the Pearse Street gates on Wednesday that two artillery pieces were brought out on the quays and put into action against the rebel outposts across O'Connell Bridge. By then, machine-guns were placed on Trinity College and from this point 'gusts of fire' swept through Westmoreland and O'Connell Streets. 'The authorities liberally sprayed all the positions held by the rebels.' [RH]

A tombstone within TCD (on the Nassau Street wall) marks the spot where Pvt Arthur Charles Smith of the 4th Hussars was killed during the Rising

A British soldier tends a comrade's grave within TCD, probably that of Pvt Arthur Charles Smith

The Custom House before the Rising

Custom House

Location: Custom House Quay
Map No. 19

Without doubt one of the finest buildings in the Dublin of 1916, the Custom House nevertheless was of no strategic interest to the rebels. The fact was that it had no military value — it wasn't a military base, nor did it overlook, or control the approaches to, any military barracks. And, as an administrative centre, it simply wasn't of great importance.

But from the authorities' point-of-view, the fact that the Custom House dominated Liberty Hall — the headquarters of the Irish Citizen Army — imbued the building with a great deal of strategic importance.

By Wednesday, the Custom House was alive with preparations for the assault on Liberty Hall. Numerous machine-gun teams were in place on the roof — and where the field of fire wasn't clear enough, parts of the walls facing Liberty Hall were simply knocked down. Below, inside the building, soldiers were ready, bayonets fixed, waiting for the order to charge across Beresford Place and capture the rebel strongpoint. Other machine-gunners were ready on the nearby roofs of Pearse Street Fire Station and Trinity College.

The final piece in the planned assault was the presence, on the quay opposite the Custom House, of the Navy gunboat, the *Helga*. Formerly a fishery patrol boat with the Department of Agriculture, and now under military command, the *Helga* brought its artillery to bear on Liberty Hall at 8 a.m. With the railway bridge in the way, the *Helga* couldn't fire directly at the building and so set its guns at an angle sufficient to lob its shells up and over the bridge.

The first one was fired — up it went into the air and then down. CLANG!

The gunboat **Helga**

shells were raining down

The shell smacked into the metalwork of the railway bridge and the sound was heard miles away.

The gunners eventually corrected their mistake and soon shells were raining down on Liberty Hall, backed up by two smaller field artillery pieces firing from Tara Street and a terrific hail of bullets from several directions. (For the outcome, see page 81.)

The Custom House was used later as a collection centre for both civilians and captured rebels. On Thursday, the fires on O'Connell Street were spreading, and staying in the area was no longer an option for the civilian population — the gunfire ceased temporarily as citizens ran from buildings carrying as much of their belongings as possible, and were directed towards the Custom House. 'Come out! Come out!' a soldier with a megaphone called to residents. Then, when the stream of refugees were out of danger, the firing resumed.

And on Friday, as bands of rebels were being captured or were surrendering, the Custom House was used as a detention centre. When one rebel officer was captured, he and his men were about to be lined up and shot in the street on the orders of a British lieutenant, but fortunately a captain happened to come around the corner.

'Where are you taking those men, Lieutenant?' he asked.

'I was going to shoot them, sir,' the lieutenant replied, but the captain then turned to the sergeant.

'March these prisoners to the Custom House, Sergeant,' he ordered. [ER]

At the Custom House, the rebels were kept in what seemed to be an air and light shaft which served a block of buildings. Throughout the night, more and more of their captured comrades were put in with them. And the rebels were surprised to find that the British officers, even before it was all over, were very eager to obtain souvenirs of the Easter Rising — 'Poor Frank Thornton, who was in full Volunteer uniform, was practically denuded of tunic buttons … [which were] courteously asked for, and he gave them up with typical good humour.' [DR]

A view of the Custom House, showing the position of the Loop Line rail bridge

I was going to shoot them, sir

Above
Troops posing beside a armoured ca

Picture courtesy Old Dublin Society

Left:
A soldier stands guard beside a ruined tram, location unknown

The Custom House today, with the International Financial Services Centre in the background.

Liberty Hall after its bombardment. Note the shadow of the Loop Line rail bridge.

Liberty Hall

Location: Beresford Place, near the Custom House
Map No. 20

'A machine-gun is turned on him. Bullets hit the pavement in front of him and behind him, they strike the roadway and the walls of the building along his route and still he runs on and on … Will he escape? He will … he won't. My God! … a bullet raises a spark from the pavement right at his toe. A hundred yards … in five [seconds] … his heart in his mouth but — safe!'

As artillery shells dropped from the sky onto Liberty Hall on the third day of the Easter Rising, reporter John O'Leary was a witness to the incredible dash for safety of the building's caretaker, Peter Ennis. [ER] But in fact that building had been a target for the authorities for years before the rebellion began.

In 1916 Liberty Hall was a much smaller building than the tower which has since replaced it. But as a thorn in the side of the authorities, it was much bigger than its actual size. It was 'the building most detested by the Anglo-Irish, the Church, the Ascendancy and the business community. It was hated with particular venom by the military and police.' [SD]

Commandant General James Connolly

Liberty Hall was the nerve centre of the trade union movement in Dublin, and it was also the headquarters of James Connolly's Irish Citizen Army — one of the two main groups which comprised the rebel force during the Rising. Inside, Connolly was making bayonets and bombs, preaching sedition and lecturing on the tactics of guerrilla warfare. Outside he had hung a banner which said: 'We serve neither King nor Kaiser, but Ireland.' So when, on Wednesday morning, artillery shells and machine-gun bullets rained down on Liberty Hall, nobody (except perhaps, the caretaker) should have been very surprised. The assault was kept up for more than an hour, while the military, convinced of the presence within of an entire garrison of rebels, fired everything they had at the building. The sound was deafening, the smoke cloud immense.

The firing stopped. The dust settled. Liberty Hall was a ruin, a mere shell — its outer walls, peppered with holes of all sizes, stood, but within the walls hardly anything remained. As for the rebel contingent … 20 British soldiers

Liberty Hall before the Rising, showing the banner Connolly had put up over the entrance. Members of the Irish Citizen Army are assembled in full uniform.

slowly advanced from the Custom House with fixed bayonets and clambered into the ruin. But if they were expecting to find bodies, they, at least, were in for a surprise.

Two days before the assault, at 11.30 on Easter Monday morning, the main force of rebels had mustered in Beresford Place, outside Liberty Hall. Those that had them wore Citizen Army uniforms of dark green or Irish Volunteer uniforms of lighter green, but most were dressed in ordinary clothes (or their Sunday best). Their weapons were just as varied — from new rifles, old rifles, antique rifles and shotguns, right through to home-made pikes. Their baggage caravan was just as varied — 'horse-drawn lorries laden with a weird assortment of weapons, boxes … pickaxes, crowbars, sledges, etc.' [DB] There was also a vegetable cart, a cab, a judge's carriage, and a van.

Connolly's statue beside Liberty Hall as it looks today

we're going out to be slaughtered

Commandant General James Connolly, seeing an old friend, went to say goodbye. 'Bill,' he said, 'we're going out to be slaughtered.'

'Is there no hope at all?' his friend asked.

'None whatsoever,' was Connolly's cheery reply.

By midday, the rebel army had marched away from Liberty Hall towards their designated positions, and only a small group of men were left guarding the building. Then, that afternoon, Connolly (by now in the GPO) ordered the complete evacuation of Liberty Hall and the transfer of any remaining supplies and munitions to the GPO. So when the shelling of Liberty Hall ended at about 10 o'clock on Wednesday morning, there were the same number of rebels inside as when it began at 8 o'clock — none.

The physical outcome of the bombardment was the complete destruction of Liberty Hall and many homes and buildings nearby, and the death and wounding of a good number of civilians. However, for the military at least, the mental effect on the rebels was satisfactory. Connolly had always insisted that the British would never employ artillery in the city, arguing that: 'A capitalist government will never destroy property.' And while some shelling had occurred the day before around Phibsborough, that could be dismissed as being 'only' the suburbs. Now, however, it was clear that the authorities were prepared to use any weapon they had in order to crush the rebellion, and the rebel morale must have been seriously bruised as a result.

Soldiers bivouacked under the Loop Line rail bridge. In the background is the bombed-out Liberty Hall. To the right, off-camera, is the Custom House.

Liberty Hall today — the tallest building in Dublin (see picture on facing page)

Looking across O'Connell Bridge, down O'Connell Street in 1916. Hopkins & Hopkins (now the Irish Nationwide) stood on the opposite corner of the bridge.

Hopkins & Hopkins

Location: Corner of O'Connell Street & Eden Quay
Map No. 21

After their 'comfortable' journey into the city centre by tram, Volunteers of the Kimmage Garrison were detailed to occupy and fortify the two buildings on the corners of O'Connell Street overlooking O'Connell Bridge. One of these corners is now a branch office of the Irish Nationwide Building Society, but in 1916 was the premises of Hopkins & Hopkins, jewellers. (See also page 89.)

Being a jewellers meant that breaking into Hopkins & Hopkins wasn't as easy as it had been with other buildings — one rebel described it as 'a tough nut to crack'. As the men were working away trying to break down the door, they were interrupted. A policeman, on duty at the bridge, approached with the intention of questioning their motives. Volunteer Cormac Turner ordered him to halt, but the officer ignored the instruction. So Turner, bayonet tip practically touching the policeman, spoke again: 'Halt or I'll run you through.'

Now the officer understood. 'Oh, I see,' he said. 'Well, you boys needn't worry about me. I won't interfere. In my opinion, it's a matter for the military.' And then he made himself scarce.

By the next day, the rebels in Hopkins & Hopkins were under constant fire from British snipers on the roof of Trinity College over the river, so since they were armed only with shotguns, they sent to the GPO for a high-calibre rifle. The rifle was duly sent, along with a crack shot rebel to do the firing.

Although the British sniping was indeed eased, the respite didn't last long. Soon other snipers were making life difficult for the three rebels in Hopkins & Hopkins. The bullets coming from TCD were joined by bullets coming from the tower in Amiens Street train station (now called Connolly Station), and by yet more coming from a shop called McBirney's on the quays across the river (now the Virgin Megastore).

the O'Connell Street area was a potential death zone

One of those bullets, however, missed its intended target and a woman walking past Hopkins & Hopkins was shot dead. Civilians (and especially looters) still hadn't learned that the O'Connell Street area was a potential death zone, and more non-combatant casualties were to follow.

On Wednesday the military had a machine-gun set up in the Tara Street fire station's tower and soon it was adding its share of bullets to the equation. Meanwhile the shelling of Liberty Hall had begun, but because of the sniper in McBirney's, the rebels in Hopkins & Hopkins had to be cautious near the windows, so they rigged up a periscope to see what was going on.

Something had to be done about the McBirney's sniper, so the rebels 'borrowed' a good pair of binoculars from the Hopkins & Hopkins stock and located his position in a central top window. The rebel crack shot was across the road in Kelly's Fort (see page 89), so the information was passed over. Then all the rebels in Hopkins & Hopkins and Kelly's aimed their shotguns — and one rifle — at the designated window across the river. The binocular man watched. The sniper appeared. 'Fire!' said the binocular man and everyone fired at the McBirney's window simultaneously.

But although that concentrated fire silenced him for a while, he hadn't gone away for good. Next day he was firing again.

A blind man walked out of a door near Hopkins & Hopkins on Eden Quay and started towards O'Connell Street, tapping with his stick. The sniper in McBirney's fired and a bullet knocked the blind man to the pavement.

An ambulance man rushed from cover, bandaged the man's wound, helped him up and led him onto O'Connell Bridge, just in front of Hopkins & Hopkins. Gunfire from both sides seemed to stop. Then, as the two men reached the

*the whole o
Eden Qua
began t
disappea*

middle of the bridge, the McBirney's sniper fired again — twice. Both bullets hit and both men fell to the ground. Finally an ambulance drove onto the bridge and sped away with the bodies.

By Thursday, the end was near for the rebels in Hopkins & Hopkins. Fires were eating towards them from Abbey Street, and to hasten matters, the British started firing incendiary bombs into the building. Within half an hour, buckets of water were useless and Hopkins & Hopkins was abandoned. The rebels ran into the back streets only to find every way blocked by soldiers. Luckily, these soldiers 'had just arrived in Dublin and weren't yet mad at anyone,' so didn't open fire on sight. Looking at the exhausted, battle-weary rebels, one soldier remarked: 'A scruffy lot, aren't they?' [AE]

Meanwhile, behind them, the whole of Eden Quay began to disappear in a huge blaze, and, at 9 p.m, Hopkins & Hopkins collapsed. Beneath the rubble, thousands of pounds' worth of gold and silver melted.

The cleaning-up begins on Eden Quay, in front of the ruins of Hopkins & Hopkins

An *Evening Telegraph* van drives across O'Connell Bridge, in front of the ruined shell of Kelly's. Note the soldier on guard on the bridge at left.

Kelly's Fort

Location: Corner of O'Connell Street & Bachelors Walk

Map No. 22

Occupied on Easter Monday by Volunteers from the Kimmage Garrison — 'armed with pikes and shotguns' — Kelly's gun and fishing tackle shop earned the nickname Kelly's Fort. (See also page 85.)

The Kimmage Garrison, led by George Plunkett, had started off walking into the city until Plunkett stopped them and said: 'Why walk when we can ride? Let us travel in comfort.' [TR] And so a tram was halted and somehow nearly 60 of them — pikes, shotguns, and all — found room on board. 'Honest George Plunkett' handed money to the conductor, saying: 'Fifty-nine twopenny fares — and please don't stop until we reach O'Connell Bridge.'

'Youse have captured the tram anyway, so why pay?' asked the tram conductor.

'We are honest men and not hooligans, and always pay our way,' was the reply.

A woman passenger lost her temper and shouted at the conductor: 'I demand that you put these men off!' The conductor, however, with nearly 60 armed insurrectionists on his tram (one close behind him with a shotgun) replied: 'In that case, would you mind doing it yourself ma'am. As you can see, I'm rather busy.'

One of the rebels inside Kelly's, Joe Good, wrote that on Tuesday most passers-by were indifferent, 'though with one exception: a man faithfully stood on the street in front of my loophole, very insistently requesting a fishing-rod he had espied.' When Good refused, the man resorted to what he presumably thought was logic: 'Sure that lovely fishin' rod will only be desthroyed, like yourself.' [ED]

The Volunteers had prepared the building for defence, smashing the windows and forming barricades with loopholes for rifles. Big books

Busy tram traffic at the O'Connell Bridge end of O'Connell Street. The picture is taken from beside Kelly's Fort, looking across at Hopkins & Hopkins, down Eden Quay towards the Loop Line Bridge and the Custom House.

and ledgers were stacked up and they 'stood up splendidly to rifle-fire, and even machine-gun fire' when it started to pour in from across the river on Wednesday.

Kelly's Fort was targeted by rifle and machine-gun fire from 'nests' set up on the tower of Pearse Street Fire Station, the roof of the Custom House, the old Tivoli Theatre, and behind the parapet of Purcell's (the triangular building on the corner of Westmoreland and D'Olier Streets).

Apart from small-arms fire, the building also came under bombardment from two 9-pounder artillery pieces brought out of Trinity College and set up on the opposite side of the Liffey — shelling began at 2.30, and the booming shattered every window in the vicinity and shook not only the GPO, but Trinity itself.

At 5 o'clock on Wednesday, the firing ceased and from the outside Kelly's didn't look too bad — apart from five shell holes in the brickwork and not one window intact. The interior told a different story however: it had been completely destroyed.

shelling began at 2.30

'Not even a fly can be alive in that house,' a man said to James Stephens after the shelling began. In fact, after enduring a solid hour of shelling, which created huge clouds of dust and tore the interior to pieces, the rebels' position was simply untenable — artillery shells couldn't be answered with rifles and shotguns. At 3.30, the order to fall back came from Commandant James Connolly in the GPO, so the Kelly's garrison left the building through the holes they had tunnelled in the walls for just that contingency.

One of the military's hastily improvised armoured cars pictured outside Kelly's Fort. Note the O'Connell monument and the ruins of O'Connell Street in the background.

91

Lower Abbey Street after the bombardment. To the left of Wynn's Hotel is the ruined shell of the Royal Hibernian Academy — a great cultural loss to the city.

Lower Abbey Street

Location: City Centre, off east side of O'Connell Street
Map No. 23

'By the left, quick march!' That was the simple order given to the rebel army standing in formation outside Liberty Hall on Easter Monday. A Volunteer officer remembered: 'We moved off at a brisk pace, swung left into Lower Abbey Street, and headed up towards O'Connell Street. We had, for good or ill, set out on a great adventure.' [DB] Just three days later, a single event in Lower Abbey Street would signal the beginning of the end for the rebellion, for the rebels, and indeed, for Lower Abbey Street itself.

But in the meantime on Monday, the GPO was occupied at noon, and soon afterwards Commandant Connolly gave orders that a barricade be constructed across Lower Abbey Street. Connolly was concerned that British troops might advance up Lower Abbey Street from the train station on Amiens Street (now called Connolly Station). A Volunteer Captain, Tom Weafer, was given the task.

At the time, *The Irish Times* had a paper store on Lower Abbey Street (now Madigan's pub) — inside, Weafer found huge rolls of paper which a team of rebels soon rolled out into the street to form the core of the barricade. Added to the rolls were furniture, machinery and boxes. A bicycle shop 'contributed' £5,000 worth of bicycles and a motorcycle — a huge sum of money in those days.

an Irish Republic has been proclaimed

When the rebels were done, the obstacle stretched over to Wynn's Hotel opposite — it was 'a formidable barrier ... the only really effective barricade in the city.' [RH] Wynn's Hotel was where, three years earlier, the founders of the Irish Volunteers first met.

Meanwhile, on the south corner of Lower Abbey Street, beside Wynn's, a Wireless School (now AIB bank) was occupied and on Tuesday a message was repeatedly transmitted to the world: 'An Irish Republic has been proclaimed. Dublin is firmly held ...' The hope was that someone at sea would hear it, but the receiver was inoperative, so there was no way to tell if they were successful or not.

By Wednesday, however, the sheer volume of bullets being poured into and around the Wireless School meant that the transmission had to be stopped.

Nonetheless, for some people, this was all just entertainment. A Volunteer on the roof of the GPO remembered looking over O'Connell Street and seeing men and women 'sitting in the windows of Wynn's Hotel in Lower Abbey Street, watching the battle as from a theatre seat.' [ER]

Later on Wednesday, rebel Leslie Price was standing at her post in the

Hibernian Bank on the north corner of Lower Abbey Street (now Irish Permanent). Standing beside her was the officer in charge, Captain Weafer, who was suddenly hit by a bullet — the wound was fatal. [WH] One source says he was shot through the lung, another says it was through the liver and kidneys. Both agree that he died a slow and agonising death. His loss turned out to be a serious blow to the rebels under his command, but worse was to come.

On Thursday morning, the British artillery was ready to start shelling the rebel headquarters in the GPO. Trajectories were set, and a field gun loaded — an artillery officer looked at his watch. At exactly 10 o'clock, the gun was fired with a boom. Its shell sailed into the air, reached its apogee, and then fell to earth again — but it missed the GPO completely, and crashed instead into, of all buildings, the *Irish Times* stores on Lower Abbey Street. In a very short time, smoke was visible from the stores and before long the building was fully ablaze. From the roof of the GPO, Pearse's brother, Willie, looked at the huge flames and said simply: 'That fire won't be easily stopped.'

suddenly hit by a bullet

After spreading rapidly to the buildings on either side of the *Irish Times* stores, the fire leaped out of that block and took hold of the carefully-built barricade across Lower Abbey Street. The paper rolls made good fuel, and within minutes the fire had moved along the barricade's entire length. Wynn's Hotel quickly succumbed to the inferno. Now both sides of Lower Abbey Street were ablaze. At the time, there had been (and still were) other fires in buildings on both Middle Abbey Street and O'Connell Street, but, four days later when the Rising was over, the Chief of the Dublin Fire Brigade spoke with hindsight of the fire that moved across the barricade: 'That was where the great fire began.'

By 11 o'clock, the blaze had found its way as far as O'Connell Street, and through the thick smoke filling Lower Abbey Street khaki-clad figures were glimpsed — now that the formidable barrier had been burned out of the way, the military were trying to advance on O'Connell Street under cover of the smoke. But smoke can't stop bullets, and, once they spotted the danger, the rebels simply poured an enormous number of bullets into the cloud at the mouth of Lower Abbey Street — so much so, that their rifle barrels overheated and had to be cooled by using the oil from empty sardine cans. The soldiers decided against a frontal assault on the GPO and retreated back down Lower Abbey Street.

But the fires raged on and, ultimately, led to the rebels' withdrawal from the GPO and the utter destruction of a huge portion of the city centre.

'As we marched towards O'Connell Street we must have presented an extraordinary spectacle,' the Volunteer officer said of Easter Monday. Less than a week later, it was Lower Abbey Street and O'Connell Street themselves which presented an extraordinary spectacle.

The ruins of the Imperial Hotel and Clery's. Here crowds are gathered to watch the remains being pulled down.

Clery's - Imperial Hotel

Location: East side of O'Connell Street, corner of Sackville Place
Map No. 24

'Many of the women were snipers, and … in the Imperial Hotel the present writer … saw women on guard with rifles, relieving worn-out Volunteers … These women could throw hand grenades, they understood the use of bombs; in fact, they seemed to understand as much about the business of warfare as their men.'

The 'present writer' was a Red Cross nurse writing anonymously in 1916. It was probably she who, on Tuesday, while the area was under fire, approached the rebel outpost beside the Imperial Hotel and demanded to be let in. Since she resolutely refused to go away, a ladder was eventually put down to her and she climbed in through a window, staying and tending the wounded until the post was abandoned.

In 1916, the Imperial Hotel and Clery's shared half a block on the east side of O'Connell Street — today the same space is occupied solely by Clery's. On Tuesday evening, the second day of the Rising, O'Connell Street had started its descent into chaos, and yet, surprisingly, some things carried on as normal — there were still guests staying in the Imperial. Just across from the hotel's imposing facade, the rebels had fortified the GPO, and the day before, several British Lancers had been shot off their horses just outside the windows — more than one horse still lay dead on the street. Meanwhile mobs looted shops up and down the street and a fire had started in a shop a couple of hundred yards away.

Nuns helping the poor

Clery's store was like an ant heap

Yet in the midst of it all, two guests went to the hotel's dining room for a meal. Soon two more men entered the hotel, but these were rebels who had come to occupy and barricade the building. However, even in a rebellion, some decorum was to be maintained — the rebel officer turned to the guests in the dining room and said: 'Finish your meal, gentlemen. There is no need to hurry. But I must ask you to leave.' The officer was probably Commandant WJ Brennan-Whitmore who was sent out from the GPO to the block opposite with orders to fortify it. 'You will defend this position to the last man,' he was told (see page 101).

By that time, Clery's was nearly stripped of everything a person (or two) could carry. One witness recalled: 'Clery's store … was like an ant heap. Men, women and children swarmed about, carrying off furniture, silks, satins; pushing baby carriages filled with sheets, stockings, garters, curtains.'

Horrified in principle, and in dismay at the effect this looting would have on the world's perception of the Rising, rebels were dispatched to put a stop to it. The mob were reluctant to leave their bonanza, and let the rebels know it: 'You dirty bowsies, wait till the Tommies bate yer bloody heads off.' Armed with rifles and police batons, however, they eventually succeeded in clearing the premises and moved on to the next looted shop. However, in every shop, the clearances lasted only until the rebel group moved on. Then the mob would return and continue looting industriously. (An English officer recalled years later that his patrol was employed 'in pulling drunken ladies from the back streets out of the cellars of various licensed premises on the Clery's side of Lower O'Connell Street with the buildings above burning away.' [IS])

great sheets of fire

At 7 a.m. on Wednesday, Commandant Connolly ordered the raising of the Citizen Army flag (the Plough and the Stars) over the Imperial Hotel (its owner was an old adversary of Connolly's). Throughout that day, machine-gun and rifle fire swept up and down O'Connell Street and into every building occupied by the rebels. But the Citizen Army flag seemed to attract more than its share of bullets and before long it was a tattered rag.

On Thursday, the end for Clery's and the Imperial Hotel approached in the form of flames. An incendiary shell landed in Hoyte's, a druggist's with an oil and chemical store just across Sackville Place (now an optician's). Soon the stores were ablaze and jets of multicoloured flames erupted from the building in every direction like a gigantic fireworks display. By 10 o'clock that evening, the whole block was burning, including the Imperial and Clery's. The rebels evacuated, some making a dash across O'Connell Street to the GPO, with loud cheers accompanying their success.

Not long after, the bulk of the buildings crashed to the ground with a huge roar and clouds of dust and smoke. And from the Imperial and Clery's 'great sheets of fire rushed high in the air.' [RH]

A side view of Clery's and the Imperial Hotel, showing the utter destruction behind the facade

Onlookers watch as the clearing gets under way in North Earl Street. The destruction of Tyler's shoe shop on the left and Noblett's sweet shop on the right was complete.

North Earl Street

Location: City centre, off east side of O'Connell Street
Map No. 25

'Occupy North Earl Street, break in and fortify the block ... You will defend this position to the last man.' With those words, James Connolly ordered Commandant WJ Brennan-Whitmore and 10 men out of the GPO and across the street. It was Monday evening and the rebels moved off, laden with rifles, crowbars and sledges.

On the right-hand corner of North Earl Street and O'Connell Street, they broke through into what was then Noblett's sweet shop (now Best's clothes shop). Upstairs they began fortifying the building — breaking glass and barricading windows. The rebels decided a barricade was also needed across the street since an attack was expected, so they began to throw furniture out into the street.

A curious crowd had gathered outside and now they gasped in astonishment. 'They're throwing away the lovely furniture, Mary. Come on!' a woman said as she picked up an armchair and started to struggle down the street with it. Brennan-Whitmore had to nip that behaviour in the bud. He ran to the street and, brandishing his automatic pistol, persuaded the woman to return the armchair.

Soon the barricade was built across the mouth of North Earl Street and fortified with wire threaded through. Connolly came over to examine it — it didn't look very strong. 'Schoolgirls could knock it over,' he declared, so he was challenged to try it. Connolly kicked it, then tried to yank a chair leg from it. The barricade held. (At some point a tram seems to have been put into service as part of the barricade — its remains are visible in the photographs.)

The curious crowd, however, quickly turned into a looting mob. A drunken cry went up; 'They're raiding Noblett's' and soon a dangerous crowd of hundreds were pushing and squeezing their way to the front of Noblett's. The glass window was shattered by the crush and immediately people were grabbing at the piles of sweets. The jagged glass made its mark on a good many grasping hands and arms — sweets became spotted with blood and still the hands reached in through the window.

sweets became spotted with blood

By the time the rebels went to fortify the opposite corner of North Earl Street and O'Connell Street, their entry was easier than before — the mob had gotten there before them. (Then it was Tyler's shoe shop, now Café Kylemore.)

At times throughout the week, however, the clergy tried (in vain) to stop the looters. A Volunteer later recalled an experience one priest told him about: 'He was hurrying down Parnell Square to where the looting was going on when he met a young bare-footed boy hurrying home with an armful of high-class boots. The good priest thought he might as well begin his work there and then. "Where did you get those boots, boy?" he demanded. The boy looked over his shoulder, but kept hurrying on. "In Earl Street, Father," says he, "but you have to hurry up, or they'll all be gone!'" [SS]

Meanwhile the rebel garrison in North Earl Street were constantly being harassed by bullets strafing O'Connell Street and the rebel positions. Snipers were a particular problem, and at one stage Brennan-Whitmore carried on a duel with a sniper on the roof of TCD which become almost personal. (See Trinity College Dublin, page 73.) At another time, they noticed a man in a window in Upper O'Connell Street who appeared to be signalling to the British artillery. He would pop his head up, look up and down the street, wave a big coloured handkerchief and duck back inside. 'Sure enough within less than half a minute a shell burst well to the rear of the post office.' A well aimed shot shattered a mirror in the 'signaller's' room and he didn't appear again.

Dublin burning! What a sight!

Occasionally a civilian would approach the men and beseech them to go on home, before they were all killed. Eventually, of course, the time did come for the garrison to evacuate the block — building after building was starting to burn and there was nothing the rebels could do to halt the advancing flames. (See Clery's - Imperial Hotel, page 97.)

Brennan-Whitmore stood on the roof of the block and looked out over O'Connell Street: 'Dublin burning! What a sight! Gruesome, awe-inspiring … Columns of deep black, evil-looking smoke spiralled up into the darkening sky. Flames leaped, twisted, curled and danced fantastically…' Soon afterwards, the North Earl Street position was abandoned.

Close-up view of the destroyed tram at the junction of North Earl Street and O'Connell Street

The ruins of the Metropole Hotel, mid-way through its demolition (see photos on page 106). The side of the GPO is clearly visible through the ruin and across Prince's Street.

Metropole Hotel

Location: West side of O'Connell Street, corner of Prince's Street beside GPO

Map No. 26

At 10 a.m, two hours before the Rising was to start, three Volunteer officers went upstairs to a room in the Metropole Hotel (now Penny's clothes shop). The junior officers were Commandant WJ Brennan-Whitmore and Captain Michael Collins. The senior was General Joseph Plunkett, one of the seven signatories of the Proclamation of the Republic. In the room, Plunkett handed automatic pistols to the other two and, with some difficulty (Plunkett was dying of tuberculosis) the three went downstairs and walked towards the street door. At the time, the Metropole was a popular lodging place for British army officers, and the hubbub in the lobby area stopped. One of the junior officers held his automatic out of sight, but with the safety catch off. Outside, the three drove to Liberty Hall.

Just a couple of hours later, the three rebel officers were outside the Metropole once more, only this time they were accompanied by 150 others — the Rising was on. Now the British officers from the Metropole were gathered on the pavement, laughing at the rebels in their various modes of uniform, with their amazing array of weapons. 'Will these bloody fools never tire of marching up and down the streets?' one remarked. After the GPO was secured, Volunteers fanned out to gather supplies, and in a very short time, the Metropole was visited — but the British officers were gone. 'Their evacuation of the hotel was as speedy as our seizure of the post office.' [DB]

Meanwhile, a Volunteer removed his hat and asked the manager: 'I must ask you to show me the way to your provisions.' 'Suppose I refuse?' the manager replied. 'If you don't co-operate, I'll take everything I find. And I'll take you too.'

Manfield's shoe shop, near the Metropole

Provisions were taken and a receipt in the name of 'The Irish Republic' was given to the enraged manager. Later the rebels returned with money to cover what they had taken, but the manager was still so angry they had to force him to take the payment.

The next time the distressed manager saw the rebels was in the very early hours of Wednesday morning. This time they hadn't come to take provisions. Now they were taking over the building — the manager just shrugged and let them at it. His wife was somewhat more concerned and asked: 'What about my personal property, my dresses, my coats?' 'They'll be perfectly safe,' a rebel assured her.

By Thursday, a tunnel had been bored beneath

the hotel, all the way up the block until the rebels could move safely into Manfield's shoe shop on the corner of Middle Abbey Street (now occupied by Clark's, another shoe shop). From here they were able to halt the military, who were trying to advance carefully up Lower Abbey Street.

During what lulls there were, the rebels in the Metropole did what they could to enjoy the plush accommodation of their surroundings — while they lasted. Thursday afternoon brought artillery shells onto the hotel roof. Volunteer Charles Saurin, on duty in the top floor, ran when a shell burst above his position, kicking up a cloud of plaster and dust. Even as he ran, another shell exploded on the roof, raising more dust and opening a huge crack in the wall. Still running, he was just about to pass by an open door, when a stream of machine-gun bullets entered through a street window and, finding no other resistance, buzzed through the open door and across his path, before peppering the wall beside him. Saurin decided to sit down and wait for a lull.

The lower floors were safer, however, including the kitchens. And, on Friday, in the middle of all the gunfire and destruction, some rebels preparing food for the garrison still retained a sense of humour, putting on the chefs' uniforms and fooling about. Of course, Friday being a non-meat eating day for Catholics, none of the still-large stock of meat was cooked.

The fooling about was short-lived however. By the evening of the same day, the military's gunners had just about found the range of the GPO — but in their 'practice' firing, they were raining shells down on the Metropole Hotel. Very

quickly the building was no longer safe to stay in and so the rebel garrison fell back to the GPO.

Not realising that it had been abandoned, however, the military continued to bombard the Metropole, switching their shells to incendiaries. The hotel began to burn and was eventually destroyed — taking with it, one presumes, the coats and dresses belonging to the manager's unfortunate wife.

a stream of machine-gun bullets

Two more views of the ruins of the Metropole, in various states of demolition.
Compare these with the large picture on page 104.

The site of the Marygold is now occupied by a clothes shop.

Henry Street lies destroyed, giving a good view of the back and side of the ruined GPO

Henry Street

Location: City centre, off west side of O'Connell Street
Map No. 27

It was Friday evening and the time had come to evacuate the GPO. After several misses, the British artillery had found its mark and shells were pounding the building. The incendiary bombs had done their work and the fires were now out of control.

By now Henry Street was under machine-gun fire from the military at the other end, but the fire in the GPO was blazing towards the basement, where the rebels had put their stores of explosives, and nobody wanted to be around when the fire finally found its way in.

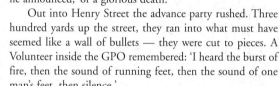

The decision was made to establish a new HQ in nearby Parnell Street, so The O'Rahilly selected a party of about 30 volunteers as the advance guard and prepared to make a dash for the chosen building. 'It will either be a glorious victory,' he announced, 'or a glorious death.'

Out into Henry Street the advance party rushed. Three hundred yards up the street, they ran into what must have seemed like a wall of bullets — they were cut to pieces. A Volunteer inside the GPO remembered: 'I heard the burst of fire, then the sound of running feet, then the sound of one man's feet, then silence.'

The O'Rahilly

Of the advance guard, only about 12 made it to anything approaching safety. The O'Rahilly himself eventually died from multiple wounds in a lane off Moore Street (the lane is now called O'Rahilly Parade). A note to his wife was found on his body, which read: 'Written after I was shot. I was leading a rush. I got more than one bullet I think.' There was a bullet hole in the note.

Meanwhile the garrison couldn't wait any longer, so at about eight o'clock, rebel Commander-in-Chief Pearse stood at the GPO's side entrance in Henry Street with his sword drawn. As he signalled with his sword, groups of rebels darted into Henry Street, through dense clouds of smoke and flying bullets, into the relative safety of Henry Place opposite.

Eventually the rebel headquarters was set up in No. 16 Moore Street, simply because Commandant Connolly was wounded and in severe pain and by then it would have been inhumane to move him any further. The final surrender wasn't far away.

Plaque in O'Rahilly Parade, off Moore Street, marking the spot where The O'Rahilly died

Henry Street had seen the last of the rebels, but the stories — some tragic, some funny — remain. Many non-combatants died in Henry Street and Moore Street during the Rising. On Thursday a civilian, trying to escape gunfire from Parnell Street, dashed from Moore Street into Henry Street, only to be killed when he ran straight into a burst of machine-gun fire. But casualties among the combatants weren't always caused by the enemy — at least one Volunteer, Henry Coyle, killed himself accidentally. He was trying to break open a door with his rifle, which was loaded and went off.

shooting over the mob's heads

Looters were also a problem in Henry Street, as in O'Connell Street, and when shooting over the mob's heads lost its persuasive ability, rebels on the roof of the GPO tried pouring buckets of water onto the crowd below in Henry Street. And even long after the rebels had left Henry Street (indeed, even after the rebellion had ended), the drama continued. Opposite Moore Street there was a theatre called the Coliseum. Part of the GPO evacuation had involved turning loose what prisoners had been taken during the week. They then had to make a run for safety and at least one was killed by gunfire from his unknowing comrades down the street.

Five days later — four days after Pearse surrendered — two soldiers were found hiding in the ruins of the Coliseum. Apparently Sergeant Henry and Private Doyle had been with the group of GPO prisoners 'turned out into the bullet-swept streets' and had eventually found safety in the theatre. And there they remained, unaware that the rebellion was over, and without food, until discovered by the manager of Bewley's (then three doors down the street).

Their ordeal (and Henry Street's) was now over and, happily, the two soldiers, 'beyond showing a dishevelled appearance were seemingly in good spirits.' [SR]

Above: the Coliseum, which stood in Henry Street, opposite the mouth of Moore Street

Left: One of the two soldiers discovered in the ruins of the Coliseum tells his tale

Henry Street today. At right is the exit from the GPO, where PH Pearse stood with his sword, directing the evacuation across the road into Henry Place (whose entrance is just visible).

O'Connell Street under fire during the Rising. Clearly visible are the Parnell monument and Nelson's Pillar — the portico of the GPO is just visible to the right of the Pillar.

The Parnell Monument

Location: Junction of O'Connell Street & Parnell Street
Map No. 28

Parnell's Monument inadvertently featured in both the beginning and the end of the rebellion as played out on O'Connell Street. On Easter Monday, it was mute witness to the first shots fired at the enemy from the GPO by the rebels. Up until then, the rebels had been fortifying the building, accompanied by 'a chorus of accidental rifle-shots which threatened to leave the British Army with nothing to do.' [ER]

A troop of British Lancers (mounted soldiers) had halted beside Parnell's Monument, while their commanding officer, Colonel Hammond, took in the situation. He decided to lead his troops down O'Connell Street in a charge against the GPO.

Inside the post office, the order was given to hold fire until the Lancers were alongside the building. The horses came galloping down the street, shoes ringing on the setts, the pennants on their lances flapping, until, as they reached Nelson's Pillar, some excited rebels, unable to wait any longer, opened fire.

Four Lancers fell from their mounts — three were dead as they fell, and one was fatally wounded. At least one horse lay dead on the street. After another volley came from the windows of the GPO, the Lancers turned and beat a hasty retreat back towards Parnell's Monument.

One of the Lancers, however, dropped his rifle as he fell and a young newspaper boy, who had been crouching behind one of the front pillars of the

three were dead as they fell

GPO, darted out, picked up the rifle, and rushed towards the rebels with it, shouting: 'Here yez are! Here yez are!' A woman tried to stop him, however, but 'the youngster raised the rifle like a club, hit her a stiff clout with it, knocking her down, continued on his way and pushed the rifle through the window to us.' [DB]

Then on the following Saturday, after seeing three people — with a white flag — being shot dead while running from a burning house, Commander-in-Chief Patrick Pearse decided that the time had come to surrender, 'in order to prevent the further slaughter of Dublin citizens.' The rebellion was ended, and on Parnell Street, within a stone's throw of the Parnell Monument, Pearse handed his sword and pistol to General Lowe. 'On the footpath, … an old wooden bench, which was used for displaying pickled pigs' heads, was brought out … here Pearse stooped and signed the document of surrender which had been placed on it.' [DR]

And, at the end of it all, 'the small band of men, who had passed through such a terrible experience, marched … to the statue of Parnell, where, in the centre of O'Connell Street, they deposited their arms.' [ICA]

Shortly after, a group of British Army officers chose the Parnell Monument as the backdrop to a souvenir photograph they had taken of themselves. The flag in the picture is the rebel flag — saying 'Irish Republic' — which, along with the tricolour, was raised above the GPO by the rebels soon after they occupied it on Easter Monday. (The officers are displaying the flag upside-down — a customary mark of disrespect to the vanquished.)

Above: Conway's pub on Parnell Street, where there is a plaque marking the spot where PH Pearse signed the surrender document. In the background, the Parnell Monument is visible — O'Connell Street joins Parnell Street at right angles.

The rebel flag which flew from the GPO during Easter Week 1916 — after correct identification by National Museum curator Pádraig Ó Snodaigh, it was returned from the UK in 1966.

Above: the front of the Parnell monument today

Left: British officers pose with the upside-down rebel flag attached to a bayonet

O'Connell Street and the back of the Parnell monument today. The GPO is more clearly visible and, of course, Nelson's Pillar is no longer there.

The GPO in ruins, above, and as it looks today, below. The flagpole from which a rebel flag flew can be seen tilted at an angle over the corner of the parapet. Note the policemen talking to an army dispatch rider.

Four of the seven signatories of the Proclamation of the Republic, all of whom were executed after the Rising.

Commander-in-Chief PH Pearse

Thomas Clarke

Joseph Plunkett

Seán MacDermott

General Post Office

Location: West side of O'Connell Street
Map No. 29

'The GPO! Charge!' James Connolly barked the order when the rebel army arrived outside the General Post Office on O'Connell Street.

There was a moment's hesitation — the fact was that not everyone who had just marched from Liberty Hall knew why they were there. Some Volunteers thought they were on routine manoeuvres. Instead here they were, armed to the teeth on a sunny bank holiday Monday, standing outside the building that was arguably the centre of Dublin itself, the GPO.

Built in 1815, the GPO had only just re-opened after a major refurbishment — it was in better condition that day than it had been for 100 years. That didn't impress the rebels, however, and so, after only a second or two, the entire band surged forward, eager for action after many uncertain weeks and months.

'Everybody out!' was the order given to the public inside the building. But the public took longer to grasp the situation than the rebels had. Then a sudden understanding swept through the citizens and a rush to the door began, such that some of the rebels even found themselves being shoved and pushed.

The GPO clock, which stopped working during the Rising

everybody out!

A woman who insisted on purchasing stamps despite the rebels milling around behind her, finally gave up when the postal clerk she'd been badgering stood up and climbed over the counter in front of her. A British lieutenant was held at the end of a pike until Michael Collins searched him, then tied him up with telephone cord and put him in a phone box, looking out onto O'Connell Street.

By then, the next order had been given: 'Smash the windows and barricade them.' Soon the interior of the GPO was filled with noise — the noise of hammers, axes, rifle-butts (whatever was heavy enough to do the job) being driven into the big window panes all around the building. As Collins himself smashed one of the windows, a woman outside shouted: 'Glory be to God! Would you look at them smashin' all the lovely windows!'

The 'lovely windows' were to prove very nasty indeed for some of the rebels — it was only a matter of minutes before one man had to rush for treatment for a gashed hand. And a couple of hours later, while dressing yet another jagged wound, Volunteer Joseph Cripps, on Red Cross duty, remarked: 'Damn those windows — they're more dangerous than the British army.'

Neither were the windows the rebels' worst enemy. In the excitement and downright confusion of the first few hours, several guns went off accidentally, some of which caused severe injuries. The rebels had also brought a big collection of home-made bombs with them, and in the afternoon one of these exploded in the face of Volunteer Liam Clarke. As he was taken to the hospital, there was amazement when the rebels saw that his face was still intact. 'So much for those bloody canisters,' said one, 'If it didn't blow Liam's head off, the divil little use it is to us.' While all this was going on, the GPO's military guard were captured without difficulty — although they were guarding one of the capital's most important buildings, they had rifles, but no ammunition.

thanks be to God, Pearse, that we've lived to see this day!

At about 1 o'clock, the rebel Commander-in-Chief, PH Pearse, went outside and read aloud the Proclamation of the Republic. The public's response wasn't very encouraging — nevertheless, Connolly shook Pearse's hand vigorously and said: 'Thanks be to God, Pearse, that we've lived to see this day!' By then, the rebel flags had been hoisted over the GPO — a green flag saying 'Irish Republic' at the left corner, and the green, white and orange tricolour (now Ireland's national flag) at the right.

The first enemy action the GPO garrison saw was when the mounted Lancers thundered down O'Connell Street, only to be shot down by a rebel volley. Several dead horses lay in the street all week, and by Thursday the stench was unbearable. (See Parnell Monument, page 113.) Even then, there was 'friendly fire'. Some rebel shots were fatally inaccurate, and at least one rebel was killed and one wounded by their comrades. Yet another rebel bullet, fired from across the street, hit the phone box where the British soldier was tied up, and it ended up in the woodwork just past his head.

During the day, rebels who had, for one reason or another, missed their mobilisation orders, started going to the GPO to join in. Two surprise volunteers, however, were a pair of Swedish sailors who said they didn't want to miss a chance to fight the English. They were accepted into the garrison, but made sure to point out that they could only fight until Thursday, when their ship was scheduled to leave port. A Spaniard somehow managed to get involved in the fighting as well, and when he needed to be treated by the medic, he caused quite a problem, since he knew no English and the rebels knew no Spanish. Finally a priest, speaking part Church Latin, part simple Spanish, managed to communicate with the enthusiastic rebel.

By Tuesday, the rebels in the GPO were more organised; there was a hospital section, food supplies were plentiful, a preparation area was designated, more home-made bombs were being made, and every rebel at the windows and on the roof had a bowlful of ammunition ready for the expected frontal assault.

POBLACHT NA H EIREANN.
THE PROVISIONAL GOVERNMENT
OF THE
IRISH REPUBLIC
TO THE PEOPLE OF IRELAND.

The Proclamation of the Republic

Among the garrison were five of the seven signatories of the Proclamation: Commander-in-Chief and first President of the newly-proclaimed Irish Republic, Patrick Pearse; Commandant General James Connolly, trade union activist and leader of the Irish Citizen Army, now in charge of Dublin operations; Commandant General Joseph Plunkett, responsible for military strategy, yet dying of glandular tuberculosis; Thomas Clarke, well-respected veteran Fenian with 15 years in an English prison behind him; and Seán MacDermott, prime mover behind the planning of the Rising. (The two signatories not in the GPO were Commandant General Thomas MacDonagh, in command at Jacob's factory, and Commandant General Eamonn Ceannt, in charge of the South Dublin Union. All seven, as well as eight others, were executed by firing squad after the Rising, while Roger Casement was hanged.)

GPO interior before and after the Rising

On Wednesday, the situation for the rebels was becoming difficult. British machine-guns and snipers were hard at work sweeping O'Connell Street, and artillery had been brought into play. Into the middle of it all stepped a 12-year-old boy, who appeared on the roof of the GPO, although he had no business there. 'Up the Volunteers!' he started to shout. 'Come on me boyos, give it to the bloody shite-heads!' And when a sniper's bullet hit the roof just beside his foot, the boy's reply was simple: 'Feck off!' Then he demanded a rifle so he could have a go himself: 'Would ye give me that gun, I'll plug a few of them feckin' limey bastards! I'll see 'em all in hell, I will!' A priest arrived on the roof then, to give conditional absolution to the rebels, and, after an enormous amount of persuasion, he finally got the boy to leave the battle-zone with him.

On Wednesday night, things were comparatively quiet, except for a drunk who zig-zagged his way from O'Connell Bridge up to the GPO. Someone inside told him to go home and so he started shouting: 'Come out, come out, will yez, an' I'll show ye! I won't go home! … Come on out an' I'll bate the lot of ye! … What do I care for the English! To hell with the English! I could bate you and them together!' Eventually he staggered around into Henry Street and faded from sight and ear-shot.

On Thursday, the end was in sight. The British artillery had set the paper stores on Lower Abbey Street alight, and the fires on O'Connell Street were only hours away from becoming uncontrollable infernos. The artillery had also scored its first direct hit on the GPO. James Connolly was seriously wounded — a sniper's bullet had shattered his ankle, but he insisted on being carried around his men's posts to encourage them — and the hospital section of the GPO was the busiest of all sections.

Watching yet another shell explode in O'Connell Street, one man turned to his comrades and said: 'Isn't this great gas, boys?' With fighters like that, the rebels' morale, at least, wasn't in much danger yet.

Late on Thursday, the fires across the street were so hot that the men in the GPO were spraying water on their barricades, but it was turning to steam. Some rebels were even pouring water on themselves. Flames were also driving rebels from peripheral outposts back to the GPO, but it too was now on fire.

Friday morning saw Connolly in bed, still unable to move his ankle, and, after dictating his final dispatch, he lay back, lit a cigarette, and picked up a book — 'What do you think of this?' he asked his orderly. 'A morning in bed, a good book to read, and an insurrection, all at the same time. It's revolution de luxe!' [AE] Up on the roof, Pearse turned to Desmond Ryan and said: 'Well, when we're all wiped out, people will blame us for everything, I suppose, and condemn us. … After a few years they will understand what we tried to do.' [TR]

Back down below, most of the women of the garrison left, but only after some intense disagreement, since they tried to insist on staying. The prisoners were also set free, and had to make their way to safety by avoiding the bullets of their comrades.

The GPO was now ablaze. Nothing more could be done — the hoses were old and a bit tattered to begin with, then holes were shot in them, and finally, the water was cut off. The confusion of earlier in the week started to creep back into the garrison. After all, they'd been five days under fire, with very little rest, not to mention the huge blazes they'd been struggling with. Bullets and shells

were coming at them endlessly, from several directions; smoke clouds filled the rooms and halls; and the noise was awful. Some guns were accidentally shot again, and more rebels were wounded. Pearse had to repeatedly shout the order to unload before everyone heard him.

Finally, the order to withdraw was given and the men gathered at the Henry Street exit (see Henry Street, page 109). Pearse raised his voice and explained the evacuation plan to the garrison, ending with: 'I want all of you to be ready to go out and face the machine-guns as if you were on parade.'

The entire garrison then sang *The Soldier's Song* (*Amhrán na bhFiann* — now Ireland's national anthem) and one by one, left the GPO behind.

The GPO and O'Connell Street in ruins, seen from Nelson's Pillar

O'Connell Street

Location: City centre
Map No. 30

Arguably the most important thoroughfare in the city, O'Connell Street was named after Daniel O'Connell, whose statue stands at one end.

Easter Monday, April 24th, 1916, saw a warming sun over O'Connell Street — it had rained for 13 of the previous 14 days, but that day the sky was blue, and, by and large, Dublin's citizens were enjoying the bank holiday. There had been rumours of a possible uprising to be staged by the Irish Volunteers on Easter Sunday, but fears had faded with the cancellation of their manoeuvres (according to a notice published in the *Sunday Independent*). Now everything was back to normal. It seemed to be business as usual.

Six days later, at nine o'clock on the morning of Sunday April 30th, some 400 tired, hungry, cold and unwashed men were lined up in formation at the north end of O'Connell Street, opposite the Parnell Monument where they had lain down their weapons the day before. Saturday night had been spent on a tiny patch of grass in front of the Rotunda Hospital across the road, crowded together, literally on top of one another in cold damp misery, with a ring of soldiers guarding them with fixed bayonets, and a machine-gun trained on them from the roof of the Rotunda.

They had fought their fight and now it was over — they marched the length of O'Connell Street towards prison. As they walked, they passed by the once-fine shops, houses and hotels that were now bombed, smashed, burned and looted. The road was littered with glass, rubbish, discarded loot, rubble, barbed wire, the remains of barricades, burnt-out trams and cars. Some fires still smouldered and smoke lingered over piles of rubble. In the middle of the road, horse carcasses rotted, giving off the very smell of death, and here and there were the marks left where civilians, or soldiers, or rebels, had been shot down in the street, in some cases to die and be left there for days, treated no better than the horses.

And all around were the pock-marks, chips, holes and gashes left by the tens of thousands of rounds of ammunition which had been fired into O'Connell

Rebel prisoners under heavy guard, being marched along the quays. Apart from the leaders, who were executed, the surrendered rebels were transported on cattle ships to the UK for internment.

Above: The ruins of O'Connell Street — this picture shows the Eden Quay corner. O'Connell Bridge is just off-camera to the right. Note the dome of the Custom House in the background.

Left: A rebel prisoner is marched along O'Connell Street

Below: O'Connell Street today

Street in the space of six days. The rebels had pressed into service practically anything that could shoot — rifles (modern, old and antique), shotguns, automatic pistols, and revolvers (but no machine-guns) and, in some posts, had kept shooting until their short supply of ammunition was spent. Meanwhile, the British military had brought the weight of a world power in the middle of a world war to bear on O'Connell Street — rifles, pistols, machine-guns, and artillery (field guns and naval guns).

And now O'Connell Street was showing its scars in silence. The guns had been quietened, but as the rebels marched that Sunday morning, the tramp of their boots broke the silence. Later would come the insults and jeers, the cries of

showing its scars in silence

'Bayonet them!' from the 'looters-turned-patriots' and the occasional lone shout of 'God bless you, boys!' (later still would come the cheering crowds as public opinion swung in the rebels' favour). But for now, the loudest sound was silence. The silence of a street that such a short time ago had being filled with the pinging of bullets, the booming of artillery, the rattle of machine-guns, the crashing of masonry, the whoops of the looters and the drunks, and the groans of the dying and wounded.

When they occupied and fortified the GPO on Monday, the rebels had been about serious business indeed, but O'Connell Street and its citizens had taken a while to realise just how serious a business it was. For many ordinary people, the start of the week was a time for fun, for letting their hair down. For cocking a snook at 'authority', for — in a word — looting.

At the very beginning, a policeman was standing looking at the GPO when a colleague approached, curious as to what those armed men milling about were up to. 'The Sinn Féiners have collared the Post Office,' was the reply. 'Bejabers, that's queer work,' said the colleague, before ambling off on his way. [AE]

Soon O'Connell Street would be entirely devoid of policemen, and would remain so until the rebellion was over and it was safe for them to go back out.

And, if there were no policemen about, and if the rebels could take what they wanted from the local businesses (rebel parties were commandeering food supplies, and leaving either cash, or receipts in the name of 'The Irish Republic'), then why couldn't the ordinary Dubliner have his or her share? And so began the wholesale looting of Dublin's most respected and famous shops.

n Fein Rebellion, Dublin
A Rebel Prisoner being
arched over O'Connell Bridge

When the rebels began smashing the glass windows in the GPO just after midday, the crowd gasped in amazement. But it was only a short time later that the crowd became a mob and began smashing windows themselves. And once they were in action, not even the powerful clergy could halt their rampage.

A contemporary postcard

Soon after the destruction began, a large number of priests arrived and tried to persuade the crowd to disperse, but to no avail. So they formed a line with arms linked and spread the width of O'Connell Street, and moved towards the crowd in an effort to drive them off the streets. Some people simply waited in side streets until the wave of priests passed on, coming out then to form another crowd behind the priests. When the clergy reached the end of the street then, they turned and moved against the new crowd, forcing them towards the other end of the street. But again, a new crowd formed in the space just cleared. 'The priests spent some time trying to achieve the impossible' before they finally gave up. [DB]

it's a mortal sin!

During the first three days of the Rising, O'Connell Street quickly became a stage on which individual little dramas were played out, as hat shops, toy shops, boot shops, clothes shops and pubs are systematically raided and looted:

- A woman sits on the carcass of a dead horse, black shawl about her head, drunk and swaying, singing;
- A scruffy boy emerges from a hat shop with four or five hats stacked on his head and the first person he meets knocks them all off his head;
- Another boy appears on the street dressed for a round of golf, from his cap right down to his plus-fours. He places a ball on the ground, selects a club from his golf bag, and swings. The ball lifts into the air and lands among a crowd down the street, as the boy, in his best accent remarks: 'Bunkered, by Jove.'
- Outside a shoe shop, two women argue over a large box of shoes, but the winner finds that they're all for the left foot;
- A young woman stands in the middle of the street with a pile of expensive underwear. She strips completely and begins to try her loot on, item by item, throwing aside whatever fails to take her fancy. The sight of a naked woman in public draws a crowd in no time. 'Would you look at the bloody hoor? Has she got no morality at all?' But some of the commentators are wearing the spoils of looting themselves, one of whom remarks: 'It's a mortal sin, that's what it is. T'Almighty God'll strike her dead!'
- Diamond rings and gold watches are auctioned by their 'owners' for as little as sixpence;
- A boy in possession of an expensive pair of binoculars offers passers-by the chance to peer at British snipers on the roof of Trinity College. 'Only tuppence a look.'

- A woman, wanting to investigate another looted shop, leaves her booty outside temporarily. When she comes out with more loot, her 'belongings' are gone. Railing at the absence of the police and their failure to protect her property, she shouts: 'The bloody place is full of thieves!'

Prisoners being transported towards the quays

Rebel prisoners march along the quays

As the week went on, however, the intensity of the gunfire increased, so the looters turned their attention to the side streets off O'Connell Street. And by Wednesday afternoon, tragedy was replacing comedy. The crowds of sightseers who had come to watch — from a distance — both the rebels and the looters were gone. The looters themselves had largely disappeared too, but since they had done their job so thoroughly, their absence was perhaps only partly to do with the increased threat of catching a bullet.

Anyone on the street was in mortal danger and an unfortunate number of civilians were indeed shot dead in O'Connell Street. Some had narrow escapes — one outrageous drunk staggered and zig-zagged his way the length of the street with impunity. Soon after, another emerged and got only a short distance towards the bridge when a bullet knocked him to the ground, where he twitched horribly for a while before lying perfectly still, dead. In a doorway in Upper O'Connell Street, a man in a top hat tried to take cover behind two pillars. Eventually a bullet found him and he 'sagged, stiffened and went down on his knees. There he remained in that curious attitude for two days. He had been shot dead, a bullet penetrating his heart'. [DN]

Finally, on Thursday, the fires that would destroy O'Connell Street were raging, and the shells sent skyward by the British artillery were seeking their ultimate target, the GPO. The pressure on the rebels approached an unbearable level. For one or two, it went past that level — one man was 'talked down' by Patrick Pearse himself, but another later dropped his rifle and ran into the street, waving his arms. And as his comrades shouted for him to return, they watched as he was shot and spun around by the impact, before falling to the ground. Then it was his turn to call out in pain to them.

And so the sheer density of bullets and bombs in the street, combined with the intensity of the blazes on both sides, meant that O'Connell Street hastened towards its final destruction, even as Patrick Pearse and the other rebel leaders were concluding that surrender was the only option left to them 'in order to prevent the further slaughter of Dublin citizens, and in the hope of saving the lives of our followers now surrounded and hopelessly outnumbered.'

The final silence slowly descended.

A rebel prisoner is marched across O'Connell Bridge — Eden Quay is in the background. This appears to be the same guard as the picture on page 123, but with a different prisoner.

Epilogue

As they were being marched along Thomas Street towards internment, an angry mob started to pelt the rebel prisoners with rotten fruit and vegetables. Abuse was thrown in even greater volume, and occasionally some citizens would try to convert their words into actions and rush towards the rebels, only to be stopped by the British soldiers and their bayonets. One rebel remembered a fellow prisoner wondering, as they marched, what would become of them. 'Do you think they might let us go?' he asked. Looking past the soldiers at the furious crowd, the first rebel replied: 'Bejasus, I hope not.' [AE]

There has always been disagreement over exactly how the opinion of Dublin's population during Easter Week 1916 was divided. Certainly the Rising had its supporters as well as its detractors, but it's probably safe to say that the majority of citizens were against the rebellion. The simple fact was that huge numbers of people were disadvantaged by the fighting and its aftermath. Women who were left to provide for families when their husbands went to fight in France were unable to collect their 'separation allowance'. Workers couldn't get to their jobs and, indeed, many were left jobless after the dust settled on their destroyed places of employment. Food was in desperately short supply during the week. For example, the many poor who depended on the Mendicity Institution for their twice-daily meal were forced to go without — and not just for seven days, but also after the fighting ended until normality resumed.

These were the things which concerned the average Dublin citizen in April 1916 — food, work, money — and it was those concerns which were being trampled on by the 'dirty bowsies' who took up arms during Easter Week. But the rebels themselves, as they saw it, had different, loftier, concerns that week. They believed they were fighting for the long-term good of Ireland and consequently, if people had to be put out in the short term, well, so be it. And there the division of opinion might well have remained, if it hadn't been for the daily news reports of executions as well as the stories of atrocities which gradually became known.

Working as fast as possible, military courts-martial were held to deal with the prisoners — 'the average time taken to hear a case and deliver a sentence was seldom more than about five minutes.' [SD] Among those court-martialled were, of course, the rebel leaders and, in the space of 10 days, 15 were shot, including Joseph Plunkett who was dying of tuberculosis anyway, and James Connolly who, because of his wounds, had to be put in a chair to face the squad. For ordering that the leaders 'of this detestable rising' face the firing squad, the British military commander-in-chief earned the nickname 'Bloody' Maxwell. In the meantime, the public were learning of the murders in North King Street (see page 32) and of the rampage of an insane English officer, Captain Bowen-Colthurst, whose barbaric acts included the summary execution of, among others, the renowned pacifist Francis Sheehy-Skeffington, as well as the murder of a boy in Rathmines, who was forced to kneel in the street before being shot in the head.

Plaque on Moore Street mark
the rebels' final F

Thus it was that, in a remarkably short time, public opinion swung massively in favour of the rebels and their lofty, yet simple, ideal — 'the right of the people of Ireland to the ownership of Ireland'. And so, when the 'dirty bowsies' were released from detention, the crowds that gathered welcomed them home as heroes and heaped praise upon them in place of rotten fruit.

Acknowledgements

Rebellion lay in his way, and he found it.
— William Shakespeare *Henry IV*

For bed, board, original source material, proofing and tolerance,
  Ursula O'Farrell.
For photography on cold, cold mornings, Denis O'Farrell.
For the gift of original material and more, Maureen Tobin.
For the loan of invaluable sources, John Cussen (and RJ Cussen).
For fact-checking, proofing, and sheer enthusiasm for the subject,
  Padraig Ó Snodaigh.
For proofing, for suggestions and for 10 of the best, Niamh Foley.
For the members' bar, John O'Carroll.
For belief and the music, Colm Ó Snodaigh.

For encouragement and prodding, all the above, plus The Family.
For postcards and forewords, Joe O'Farrell and Robert 'Bear' Tyler.
For last minute sources, Aengus Ó Snodaigh.
For taking me on, Jo O'Donoghue and Mercier Press.
For help and/or source material: Michael Kenny and the National Museum; the staff of the
  Civic Museum; the Old Dublin Society; Brian McCabe of W&G Baird; David Haugh
  of Wilson Hartnell; Rowena Neville and the Irish Museum of Modern Art; the
  National Library; Gerald Morgan FTCD; and, of course, the crew in Trinity Design.

For an appreciation (demonstrated at cost) of the necessity for the truth of the facts and the
  facts of the truth, for the first step in the journey, Myles O'Farrell, 1925-1975.

For the chance to touch history through stories, reluctantly told, of cycling through Dublin
  on Easter Monday 1916, and of taking shelter in Percy Place during the battle of
  Mount Street Bridge, and for the inspiration that came from her deep love of her native
  city, Miss Dorothy May Kerr Johnston, 1899-1993.

Finally, for sanity, for dependability in a world gone topsy-turvy, TBI.

BOOKS REFERRED TO WITHIN TEXT: *(see bibliography for full listing)*

AE = Agony at Easter	ED = Enchanted by Dreams	RH = 1916 Rebellion Handbook
CA = Capuchin Annual 1966	ER = The Easter Rebellion	SD = Six Days to Shake an Empire
CJ = Curious Journey	ICA = Story of the Irish Citizen Army	SR = Sinn Féin Revolt
DB = Dublin Burning	IS = The Irish Sword	SS = Soldier's Story of Easter Week
DFS = Dublin's Fighting Story	KG = Kilmainham Document Pack	TI = Trinity College & Irish Society
N = Dublin 1916	LW = Last Words	TR = The Rising
DR = The Dublin Rover	PA = Protest in Arms	WH = When History Was Made

Bibliography

1916 Rebellion Handbook, Mourne River Press, 1998 (Sinn Féin Rebellion Handbook, Weekly Irish Times, 1916, 1917).

Bailey, Kenneth C, *A History of Trinity College, Dublin 1892-1945*, The University Press, 1947.

Brennan-Whitmore, WJ, *Dublin Burning: The Easter Rising from behind the barricades*, Gill & Macmillan, Dublin, 1996.

Capuchin Annual, The, Dublin, 1966.

Caulfield, Max, *The Easter Rebellion*, Gill & Macmillan, Dublin, 1995 (1963).

Coffey, Thomas M, *Agony at Easter*, Penguin Books, 1971 (1969).

Coogan, Tim Pat, *Michael Collins: A biography*, Hutchinson, London, 1990.

Dublin's Fighting Story 1916-1921: Told by the men who made it, Kerryman, Tralee, 1949?

Dublin and the "Sinn Féin Rising", Wilson Hartnell & Co, Dublin, 1916.

Duff, Charles, *Six Days to Shake an Empire*, JM Dent & Sons, London, 1966.

Easter Commemoration Digest, Vol. 10, Graphic Publications, Dublin, 1968.

Fitzgerald, Redmond, *Cry Blood, Cry Erin*, Vandal Publications, London, 1966.

Fitzgibbon, Constantine, *Out of the Lion's Paw: Ireland wins her freedom*, Macdonald & Co, London, 1969.

Fitzpatrick, Georgina, *Trinity College and Irish Society 1914-1922*, Trinity College Dublin, 1992.

Good, Joe, *Enchanted by Dreams: The journal of a revolutionary*, Brandon, Dingle, 1996.

Greaves, C Desmond, *1916 as History: The myth of the blood sacrifice*, Fulcrum Press, Dublin, 1991.

Griffith, Kenneth, and Timothy O'Grady, *Curious Journey: An oral history of Ireland's unfinished revolution*, Mercier Press, Cork, 1998 (1982).

Heuston, John M, O.P., *Headquarters Battalion Easter Week 1916*, Dublin, 1966.

Holt, Edgar, *Protest in Arms: The Irish troubles 1916-1923*, Putnam, London, 1960.

Hopkinson, Michael (Ed.), *Frank Henderson's Easter Rising: Recollections of a Dublin Volunteer*, Cork University Press, Cork, 1998.

Ireland of the Welcomes, March-April, 1966.

Irish Republican Digest, The, National Publications Committee, Cork, 1965.

Irish Sword, The, Vol. VIII, No. 30, Dublin, 1967.

Irish Uprising 1916-1922, The, CBS Legacy Collection Book, Macmillan Company, New York, 1966.

Jackdaw No. 61, *The Easter Rising: Dublin 1916*, Jackdaw Publications Document Pack, London, 1969.

Kenny, Michael, *The Road to Freedom: Photographs and memorabilia from the 1916 Rising and afterwards*, Country House, and National Museum of Ireland, Dublin, 1993.

Kilmainham Gaol Document Pack, *The 1916 Rising*, Office of Public Works, Dublin, 1992.

Le Roux, Louis N, *Patrick H Pearse* (Trans. Desmond Ryan), Talbot Press, Dublin, 1932.

Maher, Jim, *Harry Boland: A biography*, Mercier Press, Cork, 1998.

MacEntee, Seán, *Episode at Easter*, Gill and Son, Dublin, 1966.

McHugh, Roger (Ed.), *Dublin 1916*, Arlington Books, London, 1976 (1966).

MacLochlainn, Piaras F, *Last Words: Letters and statements of the leaders executed after the Rising at Easter 1916*, Government of Ireland, Dublin, 1990.

National Graves Association, *The Last Post: Glasnevin Cemetery*, 1994 (1932).

Ó Broin, Leon, *Dublin Castle and the 1916 Rising: The story of Sir Matthew Nathan*, Helicon, Dublin, 1966.

O'Casey, Seán, *The Story of the Irish Citizen Army*, Journeyman, London, 1980 (1919).

O'Connor, Ulick, *The Troubles: Ireland 1912-1922*, Bobs-Merrill Company, New York, 1975.

O'Farrell, Padraic, *Who's Who in the Irish War of Independence and Civil War 1916-1923*, Lilliput Press, Dublin, 1997.

O'Higgins, Brian, *The Soldier's Story of Easter Week*, Brian O'Higgins, Dublin, 1966.

Ó Snodaigh, Aengus, *The Rotunda: Birthplace of the Irish Volunteers*, An Phoblacht, 1996.

Rebellion in Dublin, April 1916, The, Eason & Co, Dublin and Belfast, 1916

Ryan, Desmond, *The Rising: The complete story of Easter Week*, Golden Eagle Books, Dublin, 1957 (1949).

Scully, Séamus, *The Dublin Rover*, Tara Books, Dublin, 1991.

Sinn Féin Leaders of 1916, The, Cahill & Co, Dublin, 1917.

Sinn Féin Rebellion 1916, The, W&G Baird, Belfast, 1916.

Sinn Féin Revolt Illustrated, The, Hely's, Dublin, 1916.

Stephens, James, *The Insurrection in Dublin*, Colin Smythe, England, 1992 (1916).

Taillon, Ruth, *When History Was Made: The women of 1916*, Beyond the Pale Publications, Belfast, 1996.

TCD: A college miscellany, Vol XXII No. 388, June 1916

Warwick-Haller, Adrian and Sally, *Letters from Dublin, Easter 1916: Alfred Fannin's diary of the Rising*, Irish Academic Press, Dublin, 1995.